MY WINE GUIDE

(MADE SIMPLE)

GÉRARD M. SAINT-CYR

The quoted passage under the section "Wine and Health" in the chapter "Dinner Conversation" is from a course called the "World of Chemistry: Food" taught by Professor Fenster at McGill University and is printed with permission.

Images of Maps and Wine Labels © 2014 Gérard M. Saint-Cyr. Wine labels are fictitious and were designed by the author for purposes of illustration only.

Maps and Labels by Andriy Yankovskyy: yanykdesign.elance.com
Cover Design by Vesko Milacic
Roses in Vineyard image and Wine Press image © Gilles St-Cyr
Bottle and Glass Shadow image © Scot Diamond

The copyright for all other images, in the order in which they appear in this book, are from dreamstime.com as follows: © Gaultiero Boffi; © Lurii Kuzo; © Andmorg; © Hanmon; © Terrance Emerson; © Dwnld777; © Nathanphoto; © Yarchyk; © Pavlinec; © Richard Semik; © Zts; © Chiyacat; © Joop Kleuskens; © David May; © Minyun Zhou; © Pazemeckaite; © Pics1; © Kineticimagery; © Irenevandermeijs (both champagne glasses); © Paul 837; © deyangeorgiev; © Actionwatcher; © Photographerlondon; © Monkey Business Images; © Camello; © Viktorija Puke; © Ryan Carter; © Zigzagmtart; © Adeliepenguin; © Robert B George; © Marcelo Dufflocq Williams; © Jeff Halbach; © Lawrence W Stolte; © Jeanne Provost; © Elena Elisseeva; © Redlight; © Vismax; © Visuall2; © Viacheslav Silantev; © Juan DeRegoyos Sainz; © Neirfy; © Wessel Cirkel; © Creativenature1; © Richard Semik; © Igor Dolgov; © Restislav Glinsky; © Newphotoservice; © StockPhotoAstur; © LunaMarina; © Olha Rohulya; © Dekanaryas; © Richard Semik; © Boris Breytman; © Photojogtom; © Travelpeter; © Tamas Bedecs; © Radovan; © Goodluz; © Imagemakera1; © Lauren Cameo; © Jeffrey Banke; © Jborzicchi; © Kseniya Ragozina; © Jeremy Richards; © Retina2020; © Javarman; © Zimmytws; © Albo; © Vasily A. Shubochkin; © Konstantin Kirillov; © Farang; © Pleprakaymas; © Hel080808; © Shuttlecock.

Published by Mount Royal Publishing, Long Branch, New Jersey

ISBN: 978-0-692-32816-3

Dedicated to my sons Christopher and
Alexandre, whom I wouldn't trade for an ocean
of Bacchus' treasures

In memory of Catherine, Hannelore, Jim, Kat and
Gerry

Tommy,
Enjoy the book & Remember
" The best audience is
intelligent, well educated
& a little Drunk." — A. W. Barkley.
Thank you for your kindness
with me.
Cheers,
Jerry St-Cyr
3/16.

TABLE OF CONTENTS

PART II: AT THE TABLE

PART III: WINE REGIONS OF THE WORLD

PART IV: TALKING WINE

INTRODUCTION

Wine is Life!
Petronius

Wine, n. (*L.Vinum*), the fermented juice of grapes used as an alcoholic beverage.

I don't like wine—I absolutely love it. I love everything about it: the vibrant and deep colors, the heavenly aromas, the spectrum of flavors, the artful and clever labels, the various bottle styles, its stories, the geography and landscapes, the glasses and goblets and so much more. I am also particularly awe-struck when it comes to the vineyards: the history, the villages, the topography, the multitude of deep hues, the types of soil, the different canopies and best of all, the certain knowledge that at harvest time these beautiful grapes will offer the finest drink on earth.

I love wine so much I would pour a soft fruity red over my cereal in the morning!

Wine is God's nectar: Mother Nature helps vines grow in the soil, and although man and science have given her some direction—and the modern winemaker may use complex systems—the basic principles of fermentation have not changed for thousands of years.

Too many of my friends find the selecting of wine to be either too intimidating or too confusing. In fact, some friends do not like going into "sophisticated" wine stores as they are uncomfortable with the fact that they know too little about wine. In *My Wine Guide (made simple)* I hope to bring you more confidence when entering a wine store.

The same applies at restaurants. You've ordered the meals. Now what wine do you order to accompany them? Pressure! After you have completed *My Wine Guide (made simple)* you will find the world of wines very easy to navigate, and you will begin a journey into the wine world that will add to your adventures of the palate.

You need merely to open your senses in order to enjoy the full spectrum of wines. There are approximately 4,500 to 5,000 grape varieties in the world, with Portugal, Greece and Italy growing the most indigenous grapes. Interestingly, many of these intriguing grape varieties are not sold outside of their borders. I consider this most unfortunate because there are so many grape treasures that we all should have the pleasure of tasting.

As my friend Brad says, "Each time I open a bottle of wine it is a unique celebration!"

If your experiences with wine have not led you beyond Merlots and Chardonnays, rest assured that there are many delightful and high-quality wines made from other grape varieties. *My Wine Guide (made simple)* will help you to recognize these lesser-known grape varieties on labels from around the world, as well as tell you what to expect from each. We will go over many of these in the chapter titled "Grape Varieties".

I have organized *My Wine Guide (made simple)* into easy-to-digest sections, beginning with a VERY short history. In Part One I discuss grape varieties, other wine types, and the factors that affect wine. In Part Two I teach you how to taste wine, how to understand and use wine terms, and how to pair wine with food. I show you how to read and understand a wine's label and explain basic wine etiquette. In Part Three we embark upon a wine world tour, in which we explore wine-growing countries and regions. Since maps are critical to understanding wine, I have included several to help you easily comprehend the geography of wine regions. Seeing a map helps a great deal in grasping the natural aspects that affect wines, including bodies of water, mountains, latitude and longitude. I also share top vintages and my favorite wine quotes, and of course I have included a comprehensive glossary of wine terms.

There is a great deal to know about wine to really understand the subject matter in detail, and we will go over all you need to know in the following short chapters. After reading *My Wine Guide (made simple)* you will find it far easier to navigate this fascinating subject, and will start having fun with wines while enjoying each drop more and more over time.

Let's get you started on becoming comfortable with and knowledgeable about the world of God's nectar.

Cheers,

Gérard Saint-Cyr

THE GRAPES

PART I

A VERY SHORT HISTORY

Wine has been the foremost of luxuries to millennia of mankind.
Hugh Johnson

Archeological records show that ancient man enjoyed fermented fruit juice long before recorded history. Perhaps he observed prehistoric apes, elephants, or other animals enjoying the effects of eating over-ripe fallen fruits and decided to partake? Because grape juice takes only a day to ferment, it is thought that nomadic ancient man prepared and carried his primitive wine in leather skins.

Agriculture and the Vine

As man found that an agrarian lifestyle had a better calorie input to output ratio than his previous nomadic one, he began to cultivate all sorts of useful plants. In the fertile area of Transcaucasia, where Armenia and Georgia are today, man first began to cultivate *Vitis vinifera silvestris*. This vine still grows wild in that area today, but shortly after its original domestication, *Vitis vinifera* spread via trade across the Mediterranean and the Middle Eastern areas.

Soon, *Vitis vinifera* was planted in vineyards in Egypt, Greece and even Mesopotamia, where the famous Hammurabi (the "eye for an eye" guy) called wine "liquor from the mountains". Over the next several millennia, the Greeks, the Etruscans in Italy, and later the Roman Empire would spread vines and winemaking. The Romans would take wine as far east as China and as far north as England.

The Roman Empire: A Time of Advancements

The Romans were exact about many things: their social systems, their religion, their government and their wine. Roman wine was either pressed underfoot or in the newly-invented wine press. White and very sweet wine was reserved for upper-class patrons. Red wine of middle quality and second pressings was reserved for the middle classes, and the third pressings or wine that was made from water run over the leftover stems and seeds was reserved for the slaves.

Because sweeter wine sold for higher prices, honey, chalk, marble dust, leftover must and even lead was added to the wine to increase its sweetness. The wine would ferment for two to four weeks in vats that were partially buried underground to regulate their temperature.

The Roman's amazing trade and eventual military takeover of Western Europe and the British Isles allowed them to come into contact with many civilizations who shared their technologies, including the Gauls. These inventive people had access to wine prior to their contact with the Romans, and we presume they invented the wooden barrel to store beer. It wasn't until they began trading and farming wine on large scales with the Romans that they began to use their barrels for wine transport and fermentation.

Early in the Empire, the Romans not only loved wine, the people of central and southern Rome revered it with the Cult of Bacchus. From about the third century BC until it was banned in 186 BC, the Cult of Bacchus performed rites praising the god of wine and the harvest. The Empire's love of wine didn't disappear when the behavior of the cult was called into question, because the assimilation of the Jewish and Christian religions over the next two centuries would allow wine-loving religions to prosper in Rome.

The Dark Ages: Leaving Wine in the Dark

After the fall of Constantinople, the Roman Catholic Church sustained winemaking through the Dark Ages. The Church had a vested interest in wine as the Holy Eucharist, or the Blood of Christ used during Holy Communion. The maintenance of vineyards fell to monasteries in the major Catholic countries in Europe. Winemaking died out in North Africa and the Middle East where Islam grew in influence during this period.

Although winemakers were losing influence in Africa and the Middle East where they once held strong positions, they were needed in force in the New World. Spain, Portugal and France sent Catholic colonies to the New World, and they needed wine for Communion. While Florida had many native Muscadine and Scuppernong vines, the first successful U.S. vineyard was Brotherhood in New York, established 1839.

Invasion of the New World

The New World has been overwhelmingly successful at winemaking—almost to the point of actually destroying the Old World's entire vine stock. In the 1870s, a small bug, *Phylloxera vastatrix* made its way from the Americas to Europe and quickly tore through much of the French wine vines. Although they sustained less damage, Germany, Italy, Spain, Portugal, Austria, Hungary and Madeira also suffered damages to their wine industries.

Because *Phylloxera vasatrix* and American vines grew side by side for several centuries, the Old World winemakers only had one answer to their predicament: replace their ancient rootstock with newer, *Phylloxera*-resistant American rootstock. Almost all of the original Old-World rootstock was lost to the infestation and the Old World wine industry didn't recover until the 1890s.

Modern Disruptions and Innovations

Since the *Phylloxera* infestation of the 1870s, there have been a few dramatic changes in the industry: World Wars I and II wiped out many of the vineyards in Europe; the United States began producing quality wines in California; and Australia and Africa began producing wines.

One of the most interesting and unfortunate interruptions in the wine world happened in the United States from 1919-1933: the Volstead Act, or

Prohibition. For the entirety of the 1920s, manufacture, sale and transportation of alcohol in the United States were illegal and punishable under the IRS and then the Justice Department. Because of this decade-long disruption in growth and production of wine, the United States lost much ground in the worldwide wine market.

It wasn't until the mid-1900s that wine production in the United States grew to a worldwide competitive level, with central Ohio arising as the first wine region. California soon overtook Ohio in both production and quality, and by the 1970s California rivaled France with the quality of their wines. The historic 1976 Paris tasting between Californian and French wines brought the high quality of Californian wines to the world's attention. In 1979, the United States decided on the standard 750 ml bottle, which was quickly adopted by European countries for ease of trade.

Rest assured, however, these upsets have all served to produce variations in the vine that result in beautiful and interesting wines for us to taste!

GRAPE VARIETIES

Never apologize for, or be ashamed of, your own taste in wine.
Preferences of wine vary just as much as those for art or music.
Hubrecht Duijer

Grapes fall into three categories (species): European or *Vitis vinifera*; American or *Vitis labrusca*; and hybrids. Most wines of the world are made from the cultivated grape species *Vitis vinifera* and produced in Europe, Latin America, western United States, South Africa, Australia and New Zealand. Concord grapes, from the *Vitis labrusca* species, are usually made into grape juice and grape jelly. Hybrids were developed for superior hardiness and disease resistance.

The term "noble grapes" is used to describe those varieties commonly associated with the highest quality wines. Noble grapes are also known as International Varieties, because they are widely planted in most of the major wine-producing regions throughout the world with widespread appeal. Some enumerate twenty noble grapes while others name up to six. I define the eight varieties of noble grapes as follows:

Red Grape Varieties: Cabernet Sauvignon, Merlot, Pinot Noir, Syrah

White Grape Varieties: Chardonnay, Riesling, Sauvignon Blanc, Pinot Gris

Each of these eight varieties is discussed in the following chapters, in addition to a number of other noteworthy grapes from around the world.

RED GRAPES

Pinot Noir

Burgundy, France is the original home of this temperamental grape where, due to the possibility of hail and early spring frost, red burgundy (made from Pinot Noir) is the most difficult wine in the world to make with success. You will find delicious Pinot Noir wines from Oregon, California (Remember the movie *Sideways*?) and Washington in the United States. In Canada, Pinot Noir is grown in Ontario and in British Columbia.

Pinot Noir grapes are grown in cooler regions around the world including Austria where it is known as *Blauburgunder*, Germany where it is *Spätburgunder,* and Switzerland. Pinot Noir is also cultivated in Australia, Italy, New Zealand, Spain and South Africa. Pinot Noir is one of the primary varieties (along with Chardonnay and Pinot Meunier) used in the production of Champagne.

Pinot Noir grapes are light in color, with low levels of tannin and very thin skin. The plant is both rot-prone and susceptible to viruses.

Pinot Noirs usually possess a smooth texture and velvety finish. They have a red fruit character of strawberry, raspberry, cherry, plum and cassis, with vegetal and some animal nuances. They are best consumed young, within two to eight years, though Grand Cru-classified Burgundy can age 8 to 25 years.

Pinot Noir is a very versatile food wine. It is great with poultry, salmon, tuna, mildly prepared beef, duck, ham, quail, pheasant and vegetable dishes.

Merlot

Merlot is the main grape of Saint-Émilion and Pomerol on the Right Bank of Bordeaux in France. It is also grown in Languedoc-Roussillon in the South of France, California, Chile, Argentina, South Africa, Italy (Tuscany) and Spain (Navarra). Merlot requires a moderate to a hot climate.

Merlot is lighter in color, acidity and tannins than Cabernet Sauvignon, and it also has more body and more alcohol than Cabernet Sauvignon. Merlot is soft, rich, round and fruity, with a smooth, mellow feel in the mouth that is very popular in North America. Oak barrels are often used to age wines, and they give Merlot a warm, woody character. Some of the flavors of the wine combined with the barrel give vanilla, coffee, mocha, butter and/or caramel notes. Merlots from moderate climates have a red fruit (red berry, strawberry and red plum) character, while Merlots from hot climates have a black fruit (blackberry, black plums and black cherry) character. Merlot is best consumed within two to ten years, though Classified Bordeaux can age from eight to twenty-five years.

Merlot is excellent with dishes such as beef, duck, veal and pork. It also goes well with tuna and salmon.

Cabernet Sauvignon

Cabernet Sauvignon is the primary grape of the top vineyards on the Left Bank of Bordeaux. It is also found in Southern France, California, Chile, Argentina, South Africa, Italy (Tuscany) and Spain (Navarra). DNA evidence has shown that Cabernet Sauvignon is actually a cross between Cabernet Franc and Sauvignon Blanc. Cabernet Sauvignon needs a moderate to hot climate.

Cabernet Sauvignon is deeply colored with high levels of tannins and acidity. Wines made with Cabernet Sauvignon are suitable for aging and oak is often used to age these wines. Expect a black fruit character (black currant, black cherry and raspberry) with bell pepper, light mint, light chocolate, cedar and tobacco notes. Cabernet Sauvignon is best consumed in four to twenty years, though Classified Bordeaux can age from eight to twenty-five years.

Cabernet Sauvignon complements robust red meats such as beef, venison, bison, duck, lamb, pheasant and roast chicken, as well as tuna when served rare.

Cabernet Franc

Cabernet Franc is primarily grown in Bordeaux and the Loire Valley in France. It is believed to have been planted in the southwest of France in the 17th century. Cabernet Franc is a Bordeaux grape usually blended with Cabernet Sauvignon and Merlot. Some of the most expensive red Bordeaux wines from the Right Bank, however, contain more than 45 percent Cabernet Franc. A very important grape variety, it is vinified alone in the Loire Valley. Cabernet Franc is also grown in Italy, Spain, the United States, Australia, South Africa, Canada, Chile, Argentina and New Zealand.

Red Grapes at Harvest Time

Cabernet Franc is medium bodied, with blackcurrant, raspberry, plums, herbaceous, vegetal, leather, earthy, oak and cedar notes. It is best consumed in four to twelve years.

Cabernet Franc is best paired with grilled vegetables like eggplant and zucchini and tomato-based dishes. It also accompanies lighter meats such as chicken, turkey, smoked ham, pork tenderloin, veal and grilled salmon as well as game birds.

Syrah

Known as Shiraz in Australia, Syrah gained its reputation in France's southern Côtes du Rhône region. To grow properly, Syrah needs a moderate to hot climate.

Syrah is deeply colored, with medium-high levels of tannins and acidity. It is usually rich, full-bodied and age-worthy, and oak barrels are often used to age these wines. Syrah has a black fruit character (blackberry, black currant) with dark chocolate, licorice flavors and black pepper spice. Vegetal, herbal, leathery, oak and smoke notes develop with age. Syrah is best consumed in four to sixteen years.

Note: Shiraz is the Syrah grape of the Rhône Valley in France. They are viticulturally identical, but due to the different *terroir* and climates the Australian Shiraz is sweeter, riper and more chocolate than the Rhône Syrah which is spicier with a soft pepper note. The Australian name Shiraz comes from the medieval capital of Persia.

Syrah pairs well with brisket, beef steak, stew, lamb, venison and pork chops.

Grenache

Grenache originated in Garnacha in Spain and is widely grown in southern Côtes du Rhône. It is used for the production of rosé wines in Spain and France. Grenache needs a hot and dry climate to ripen.

Grenache is light in color, medium to full-bodied with high levels of alcohol. It has a red fruit character (strawberry, raspberry and blackcurrants) and mild spices (pepper, clove and licorice). Grenache is best consumed in two to eight years.

Serve Grenache with grilled meats, hamburgers, sausages, steaks, roasted pork and lamb, stews, game, duck and pheasant. It can also blend well with rich, tomato-based pasta dishes and moderate to highly spiced dishes. Grenache is not recommended with seafood.

Gamay

Gamay is from the Beaujolais and Loire regions in France. In the Loire Valley, the best Gamay wines are from the Chinon and Bourgueil regions. The Gamay grape dates back to around 1360 AD and it is thought to be from the French village of Gamay. Gamay Noir is a cross of Pinot Noir and the ancient white variety *Gouais*.

Gamay is also used to make Beaujolais, a wine produced in the Beaujolais area of France, which is part of the southern Burgundy region. The ten Beaujolais Crus from north to south include: Saint-Amour, Juliénas, Chénas, Moulin-à-Vent, Fleurie, Chiroubles, Morgon, Régnié, Brouilly and

Côte de Brouilly. The fullest-bodied Beaujolais are Chénas, Juliénas, Morgon and Moulin-à-Vent, and they are well worth a try.

You can now taste some lovely Gamay wines from the Willamette Valley in Oregon, the Columbia Gorge in Washington State and the Niagara Peninsula in Ontario. A small number of wineries in Australia have also started growing Gamay.

Gamay is light in tannin, light to medium in body, and offers red fruit/berries and sour cherry flavors with light notes of peach and banana. It is best consumed "young"; within one to three years. Case in point, Beaujolais Nouveau is so-called because *nouveau* means "new" (i.e., young) in French.

Gamay is best paired with turkey, lamb, sweet pork, lightly spiced chicken dishes, grilled salmon and *charcuterie* (cold cuts).

Nebbiolo

Nebbiolo is a large, black grape responsible for some of the finest and longest-lived wines in Italy, primarily in the North Piedmont region. The name is derived from the Italian word for fog, which is present in October during harvesting. Barolo and Barbaresco are the regal wines using Nebbiolo. Barolo is often called "the king of Piedmont" and Barbaresco "the queen of Piedmont".

Nebbiolo is very aromatic and complex. It expresses a fullness of flavor, which balances the acidity and substantial tannins. It contains notes of violet, plum, cherry, truffle and, with age, smoke and tar.

Nebbiolo complements braised short ribs, beef roasts, stews, full flavored lamb and anything with truffles or truffle oil. It is not recommended for seafood, chicken or pork.

Sangiovese

Sangiovese is the main red grape grown in Tuscany, Italy and is the primary component of the Chianti blend. The name comes from the Latin *sanguis Jovis* meaning "the blood of Jove". One of my favorite wines, Brunello di Montalcino, is made of the very best Sangiovese grapes. Super Tuscans are predominantly made of Sangiovese. Sangiovese is also grown in Argentina, France, Greece, Switzerland, the United States and Canada.

Sangiovese has high acidity and light body and is best consumed in two to eight years. When Sangiovese is young, there are fresh fruity flavors such as strawberries, as well as rose petals with light spicy notes. When Sangiovese is aged, it is hearty and dry with black cherry and plum along with vanilla, oak and sometimes a light tar note.

Sangiovese goes well with steaks (rare to medium rare), roast beef, roasted game birds, rich chicken or mushroom dishes, stuffed green peppers and of course anything with tomato sauce. Sangiovese also goes well with Veal Scaloppini dishes. The lighter Chiantis go well with seafood.

Tempranillo

Tempranillo is Spain's answer to Cabernet Sauvignon. You'll note the soil in parts of Spain is very arid and these hardy grapes grow beautifully here. *Temprano* means "early" in Spanish and the Tempranillo grape ripens early in the growing cycle. The grapes are thick-skinned and capable of making deeply colored, long-lasting wines that are not very high in alcohol.

It is worthy to note that Tempranillo is the mainstay of Spain's most respected red wines from the regions of Rioja and Ribera del Duero. Portugal produces beautiful Tempranillo wines where it is known as *Tinta Roriz*. Tempranillo vines have also been successfully adopted in California, Argentina and Australia.

Blue Grapes on a Vine

Notes are strawberry, berries, plum and herb with some spices, light leather, vanilla and fresh tobacco elements. Tempranillo is best consumed in two to eight years.

Serve Tempranillo with meat dishes such as lamb stew, beef, roast chicken, quail, large fish steaks such as swordfish and shark, Mexican,

Mediterranean and, of course, Spanish foods. A light Rioja will go with medium- flavored seafood.

Pinotage

Pinotage is a hardy and increasingly popular red grape variety that is South Africa's interesting offering to the world of the *Vitis vinifera* vine. Grown almost exclusively in South Africa, Pinotage today can also be found in New Zealand, Germany and the United States.

It is not to be confused with Pinot Noir. In 1925, scientists at Stellenbosch University crossed the grape variety Pinot Noir with Cinsault (Cinsaut in South Africa) to create the hybrid Pinotage. As Cinsault was originally known as Hermitage in South Africa, when it was crossed with Pinot Noir the two names were contracted into Pinotage. Pinotage prefers hot or moderate climates.

Pinotage grapes produce rich, long lasting, gamey, deeply colored wines with wild, fruity berry, meaty animal and earth-driven notes followed by smoke. It can at times present itself as having a sweet pungent odor. It is medium to full-bodied and high in alcohol. Pinotage is best consumed in five to sixteen years.

Try Pinotage with dishes like smoked duck, pulled pork and beef. It goes well with Mediterranean dishes including green and red peppers and eggplant. It also pairs well with Indian curry, barbecue sauces and chili con carne.

Malbec

Malbec is a black grape variety once popular in the Bordeaux region of France. Today it is associated with Mendoza, Argentina and Cahors (a small area in the Rhône Valley) and, to a lesser extent, the Loire Valley. In fact, today Argentina leads the world in Malbec production, with over 75 percent of the world's acres of Malbec. This grape variety is becoming more popular throughout the world and offers some very interesting characteristics. It is certainly worth tasting.

Malbec has medium tannin. It is best consumed within three to fifteen years. French Malbec shows blueberry, cherry and plum notes and is a tad earthy with vanilla and mocha. Argentine Malbec can have a ripe, lovely berry taste, be soft textured and lush and is capable of extended ageing. Oak and vanilla are more prominent.

Malbec complements barbecued ribs, BBQ chicken, prime rib roast, roasted beef tenderloin, grilled pork, gamey fowl, duck and, yes, ostrich.

Xynomavro

Xynomavro is a black grape variety grown in Northern Greece as far South as the foothills of Mt. Olympus. Its name means "acid black" and the wines can often seem harsh in their youth, but they age very well, as mature Naoussa can demonstrate. Looking for something different? Try a Xynomavro. I am confident that you will enjoy the adventure. I especially love this grape with Greek cuisine.

Xynomavro has powerful tannins, high acidity and complex flavors of cinnamon, black licorice, vanilla and wood, similar to a softer Barolo. It is best consumed in four to ten years.

Serve Xynomavro with Greek food such as Spanakopita, Moussaka and Pastitsio and, of course, a leg of lamb *à la Grecque* or Greek style. It is also exceptional with other Mediterranean cuisines.

Zinfandel

The Zinfandel grape is the pride of California, where 95 percent of the world's Zinfandel is grown. The remainder is grown in South Africa, Italy and Australia. Primitivo from Italy is identical to Zinfandel, and the wine served at the Last Supper is said to have been Primitivo.

Zinfandel grapes make robust, hearty and spicy reds. Zinfandel is a big, fruity, full-bodied wine with a mixture of dark fruit such as blackberry, raspberry, cherry, plums, raisins, spice and black pepper along with oak notes. It has plenty of tannins and alcohol and is best consumed in two to six years.

Zinfandel goes well with beef stew, BBQ chicken, chili, tuna, quail, pheasant, brisket, BBQ Italian sausage, Cajun and Asian cuisine.

Ripening Zinfandel Grapes

WHITE GRAPES

Chardonnay

The reputation of this noble white grape was established in Burgundy and it is France's most famous white grape variety. The sparkling wine Champagne is made of Chardonnay, Pinot Noir and Pinot Meunier. Chardonnay is also grown in a wide variety of climates and regions throughout the world including California, Canada, Australia, New Zealand, South Africa, Chile, Argentina, Austria, Italy, Germany, Switzerland, Portugal and Spain (Navarra Region). Chardonnay can be grown in cool, moderate or hot climates.

Chardonnays produced from grapes grown in a cool climate have a high natural acidity, with citrus, apple, pear, vegetal and buttery notes. Those grown in a moderate climate have a white stone fruit (peach) character, with citrus and hints of melon. Chardonnays cultivated in a hot climate have tropical fruit (pineapple, banana, mango, honey fig) and light vanilla notes. Chardonnay is best consumed in two to six years.

Chardonnay enhances lobster, flavorful fish, shrimp, chicken, turkey and pork. Heavily oaked Chardonnays pair well with smoked fish and spicy Asian cuisine.

Sauvignon Blanc

Sauvignon Blanc is one of the big white wine grapes native to the Loire region in France and is France's second most important white wine grape variety. It is also grown in California, Italy, Australia, South America and New Zealand, which produces gorgeous Sauvignon Blanc in part due to its perfect climate. Sauvignon Blanc prefers cool, moderate climates.

White Grapes on Old Vine

Sauvignon Blanc has high levels of refreshing acidity and a pungent, vegetal, aromatic character. It is very crisp, with green fruit, citrus, grapefruit, gooseberry, fresh-cut grass, lime, elderflower, bell pepper and asparagus notes. It is best drunk when young (within two to five years). Most are not aged in oak, but the best and often oak-aged versions can age from five to fifteen years.

Sauvignon Blanc is best paired with crab, oysters, scallops, shrimp, mussels, chicken and pork.

Riesling

Riesling is native to the Rhine Region of Germany, with beautiful examples also found in Alsace, Canada and the United States. It is also grown in Austria, Northern Italy, Australia, New Zealand, Chile and South Africa. Riesling prefers cool, moderate climates.

Riesling has an aromatic, fruity, floral character with crisp minerality and sometimes light spice scents. It can come in a range of styles from bone dry to lusciously sweet. Cool climate Rieslings have notes of green fruit, fresh apple, pear and citrus fruit, while moderate climate Rieslings have notes of citrus and stone fruit, peach, apricot and fresh lime. High levels of acidity help these wines age in the bottle, but if aged too long, they can develop petrol-like aromas. Rieslings are best consumed in two to thirty years.

Cool climate Rieslings go well with ham, oysters, lean shellfish and veal. Moderate climate Rieslings pair well with pork, chicken, medium-flavored fish and lobster. It can also be enjoyed with Thai and Chinese cuisines that are not too spicy.

Gewürztraminer

Gewürztraminer is one of the great European white grapes. It is planted in France's Alsace Region and in Germany, Austria, Hungary, Italy, Australia and New Zealand. It is also grown in New York and the Niagara Peninsula in the province of Ontario. The grape's skin is actually pinkish red.

Gewürztraminers are full-bodied and crisp. They can be off-dry to late harvest sweet and are best consumed in five to twenty years. Gewürztraminers are very aromatic with tropical fruit such as mango and pineapple. Other notes include roses and pears, as well as spices of cinnamon, light cloves, ground pepper and soft nutmeg. Gewürztraminer is known as "the spicy white".

Gewürztraminer pairs best with spicy chicken, duck, turkey, pork, medium to full-flavored fish, shrimp and crab. It also goes very well with spicy Indian, Middle Eastern and Chinese foods.

Pinot Gris/ Pinot Grigio

Pinot Gris and Pinot Grigio are the same grape variety. It is thought to be a mutant clone of the Pinot Noir grape. Grown primarily in Alsace, France and Germany, Pinot Gris can also be found in New Zealand, Tasmania, Australia, Washington and Oregon. Pinot Grigio is found in Northeastern Italy.

Pinot Gris/Pinot Grigio is very popular as a "beginner's wine", since it is light and very accessible. It has medium to medium-high acidity, with lime, pear, green apple, melon, lemon, white nectarine and white peach notes. Wines made from French grapes are rich, fat and sweet, while those made from Italian grapes are light, crisp, clean and dry. Pinot Gris/Pinot Grigio is best consumed within one to three years.

Pinot Gris/Pinot Grigio complements light fish such as tilapia, sole, trout, cod, halibut, mussels, scallops, oysters, chicken, turkey, ham, veal, Italian antipasti and light pasta.

Sémillon

Sémillon is one of the major white wine grape varieties native to the Bordeaux region of France and France's third most important white grape.

It is also grown in Australia, New Zealand, the United States, Argentina and, to a lesser degree, in Chile and South Africa.

Sémillon is susceptible to Noble Rot or Botrytis, a fungus which affects many plant species and which concentrates the sugars of late harvest grapes. When blended with Sauvignon Blanc it creates exceptional wines, especially the world-class sweet wines of Bordeaux, like Sauternes.

Sémillon gives wines body and a beautiful golden color. They can be dry to very sweet, with green apple, lime, grapefruit, mango, grass, gooseberry, asparagus and raisin to

Noble Rot

honey notes with a high acidic side. Sémillon is best consumed in five to fifteen years.

Serve Sémillon with chicken, pork chop, ham, turkey, foie gras and duck. Also try medium-flavored fish such as trout, arctic char, red snapper, halibut and Chilean sea bass. Indian and other Asian cuisines are suggested as long as they are not too spicy.

Chenin Blanc

Chenin Blanc is also known as Pinot de la Loire in the Loire Valley, France. The white wines of the Anjou AOP are a special expression of Chenin as a dry wine and in the nearby Vouvray AOP the style is more off-dry. Please see page 97 for more information about AOP. Chenin Blanc is grown from China to New Zealand, Canada, California and Argentina. It is also the most widely planted grape variety in South Africa, where it is known as Steen.

Chenin Blanc can be very dry to sweet, with green apple, lemon, stone fruits such as peach and apricot, angelica, honey, nut and floral notes. It is worth noting that South African Chenin Blanc tends to be crisper and zestier in style than that produced in the Loire Valley. Chenin Blanc is best consumed in four to thirty years.

Chenin Blanc goes well with veal, cream-based chicken dishes, turkey, pork chops, halibut, smoked salmon and paté. Try it with Chinese cuisine. Oaked Chenin Blanc goes well with foie gras.

Viognier

Viognier has been historically grown in the Condrieu region of Northern Rhône in France. It is also grown today in Southern France. Other production is found in California, South Africa, Australia and, to a lesser degree, in Oregon, Washington and New Zealand.

Flavors include apricot, pear, ripe peaches, honeysuckle, citrus blossoms and light musk. Viognier is best consumed in two to five years.

Pair Viognier with chicken, turkey and seafood such as scallops, crab, lobster, clams and fish such as sturgeon and trout. Do not pair with lighter foods. Try it with Indian cuisine as well.

Grüner Veltliner

Grüner Veltliner, which means "green grape from the village of Veltlin", is a white wine grape variety grown primarily in Austria and is Austria's signature grape variety. It is also cultivated in Hungary, Slovakia and the Czech Republic and can be found in numerous states in the United States as well as in Australia and Canada. The grapes are deep green in color. This grape variety is generally overlooked and yet it is such a treat. I strongly recommend you taste this variety, especially if you want something new and different.

Grüner Veltliner is usually a dry wine with apple, peach, citrus, lime, nectarine, lentil and celery flavors with white pepper spice. It is best consumed in two to twenty years.

Serve Grüner Veltliner with Wiener Schnitzel (of course), pork tenderloin, smoked ham, turkey, sushi, seafood and Vietnamese and Thai foods.

WINE SCALE FROM LIGHTEST TO HEAVIEST

A waltz and a glass of wine invite an encore.
Johann Strauss

I love classical music, and when listening to it I often think of the style of each composer as falling on a scale of lightest to heaviest, in much the same way that I categorize the lightness or heaviness of wines. I think of Vivaldi as a Pinot Grigio; the composer's music sounds light and smooth and the wine drinks easily. Wagner, on the other hand, is a Borolo: strong, complex and cerebral.

Here is how I rank some of my favorite composers, from the lightest touch and softest tone to the strongest touch and deepest tone: Vivaldi, Pachelbel, Haydn, Handel, Chopin, Tchaikovsky, Brahms, Bach, Mozart, Beethoven, Rachmaninov, Wagner.

Similarly, here is how I classify the wines discussed above, from lightest to heaviest. Think of this scale as shorthand to help you identify the kind of wine you are looking for.

Whites: Pinot Grigio, Riesling, Muscadet, Champagne, Grüner Veltliner, Sauvignon Blanc, Sémillon found in Bordeaux, Sancerre in the Loire Valley, Unoaked Chardonnay in Mâcon, Gewürztraminer grown predominantly in France and Germany, Oaky Chardonnay in the United States, Burgundy Chardonnay and Côtes du Rhône whites.

Reds: Beaujolais, Dolcetto, Côte de Beaune Pinot Noir, Rioja, East Bank Bordeaux where Merlot is predominant, Northern Burgundy/Côte de Nuit Pinot Noir, Malbec, West Bank Bordeaux where Cabernet Sauvignon is predominant, Zinfandel, Côtes du Rhône reds, Syrah/Shiraz, Barolo.

OTHER WINE TYPES

Champagne, the great civiliser.
Talleyrand

It is not commonly known that Port, Madeira, Cognac, Armagnac and Sherry are all made from fermented grapes and are therefore classified as wines. They are "fortified", which means that a distilled spirit, usually brandy, has been added to them in the proportion of one part spirit to four parts wine.

All of the wines in this section are what are known in France as *apéritifs* and *digestifs*: alcoholic drinks served with meals. Apéritifs are served before the meal to stimulate the appetite; digestifs are served after the meal to aid digestion. Sparkling wine is usually consumed as an apéritif before meals, but I do have some friends who enjoy sparkling wine through dinner and afterwards. Port, Madeira, Cognac and Armagnac are all after-dinner drinks, though Madeira and Port are occasionally consumed before dinner. Drink Port alone, or as a perfect accompaniment to dessert. This is true of Sherry as well, depending on its sweetness.

Fortified wines like Port, Sherry and Madeira have a much longer shelf life once they've been opened than regular wines, due to their high alcohol and, in some cases, high sugar content. These elements act as preservatives and give fortified wines much more longevity than non-fortified wines. The shelf life of an opened bottle of fortified wine will vary depending on the specific wine type.

Sparkling Wines

A fun bit of information is that the bubbles in sparkling wines are called "pearls". It is often said that the smaller the pearls, the finer the sparkling wine. Perhaps.

Sparkling wines are made from a variety of different grapes: Pinot Noir, Chardonnay, Pinot Meunier, Pinot Blanc, Riesling, Mauzac, Chenin Blanc, Cabernet Franc, Macabeu, Xarel-lo, Parellada, Pinot Noir, Shiraz, Muscat Blanc à Petits Grains and Müller-Thurgau. As Jean-Marie Barillere, CEO, Champagne Mumm pointed out: "…the base of everything is, truly, the grapes."

The sparkling wine scale from driest to sweetest is as follows: Brut Nature, Extra Brut, Brut, Extra Sec/Extra Dry, Sec/Dry/Seco/Secco/Trocken, Demi-Sec/Rich/Halbtrocken/ Semi-Dulce/Abbocato, Doux/Sweet/Dolce/ Doce/Dulce.

CHAMPAGNE

True Champagne is produced only in the Champagne region of France and is made of Chardonnay, Pinot Meunier and Pinot Noir grapes. Some of the finest Champagnes are actually rosés. Note that Blanc de Blancs Champagne is made completely of Chardonnay. Blanc de Noirs Champagne is made from Pinot Noir, Pinot Meunier or a blend of the two.

CRÉMANT

The term Crémant is used to designate sparkling wines made by the *méthode champenoise* in France, but made *outside* the boundaries of the Champagne region. Crémants are also made from grapes other than the traditional Champagne varieties. Crémant d'Alsace, for example, is made from Pinot Blanc, Riesling or Pinot Gris.

SEKT

Sekt, sparkling wine from Germany, Austria and the Czech Republic, is usually made from Riesling, Pinot Blanc, Pinot Gris and Pinot Noir grape varieties.

CAVA

Cava is sparkling wine from Spain and is made from Xarel-lo, Macabeo and Parellada grape varieties.

ASTI SPUMANTE/PROSECCO

Asti Spumante/Prosecco is sparkling wine from Italy and is made from the Glera grape variety (formerly named Prosecco).

SPARKLING WINE IN THE UNITED STATES

In the past, sparkling wine in the United States was made from Riesling, Muscatel, Traminer and Chasselas grapes. California sparklers improved their quality by introducing the more traditional Chardonnay, Pinot Noir, Pinot Meunier and Pinot Blanc grapes.

ESPUMANTE

In Portugal, sparkling wine is called Espumante. It is traditionally made using red Baga or Touriga Nacional grapes and white Fernão Pires (Maria Gomes), Arinto and Bical grapes, though today Chardonnay and Pinot Noir are used more often.

SOUTH AFRICAN SPARKLING WINES

South African sparkling wines made in the traditional French method (méthode champenoise) are referred to as Méthode Cap Classique or MCCs and the grapes used are Sauvignon Blanc, Chenin Blanc and, in some cases, Pinotage. The use of Chardonnay and Pinot Noir is on the rise today.

Sweet or Dessert Wines

Dessert wines are so called because they are usually enjoyed after dinner. These wines are best consumed in five to thirty years, but top Sauternes can last up to one hundred years. Dessert wines are best served with fruity, sweet desserts, ice cream and sorbets.

Sauternes, Barsac, Bommes, Fargues and Preignac of Bordeaux, France are made of Sémillon, Sauvignon Blanc and Muscadelle grapes. The French villages of Cadillac, Loupiac, Sainte-Croix-du-Mont, Cérons and Premières Côtes de Bordeaux produce other excellent sweet wines with a more affordable price tag than true Sauternes wines. Muscat de Beaumes-de-Venise (Southern Rhône, France) is made of Muscat grapes. Tokaji (Tokaj region, Hungary) is made of Furmint, Hárslevelű and Muscat Blanc grapes. Hungary instituted the measurement of sugar on the label of dessert wines to denote the level of sweetness, counted in Puttonyos.

Number of Puttonyos	Grams of Residual Sugar Per Liter
3	60
4	90
5	120
6	150

Aszú Eszencia has 180 g of residual sugar per liter. It is one of the rarest and most expensive bottles of wine in the world and very much worth trying. Aszú Eszencia, often called a nectar, is best consumed in five to thirty years, but some of the best can age up to one hundred years. I have even read of a bottle of Aszú Eszencia that was opened after two hundred years—absolutely mind-boggling!

Vin Santo or Vino Santo means Holy wine (Italy). It is traditionally from Tuscany and often made from white grape varieties such as Trebbiano and Malvasia. These wines must have a minimum alcohol level of 15 percent and be aged for at least three years prior to release.

Other sweet wines worth mentioning are Sciachetra, Recioto di Soave, the red Recioto della Valpolicela from Italy and straw wine from the Jura, Rhône and Alsace regions of France.

If you enjoy sweet dessert wines such as Sauternes I strongly suggest you taste these above-mentioned wonderful drops.

Icewine/Ice Wine/*Eiswein*

Icewine, Ice Wine and *Eiswein* are expensive, as all harvesting is done by hand. The grapes may stay on the vine for several months following the normal harvest period. In Canada, the United States, Austria and Germany, the grapes must freeze naturally to be called ice wine. The temperature must be 17°F/-8°C or colder. If a freeze does not come quickly enough, the grapes may rot and the crop will be lost. The longer the harvest is delayed, the more grapes will be lost to animals and fallen fruit. The grapes are typically picked at night or in early morning and pressed immediately.

Ice Wine Grapes

Canada is the largest Icewine producer in the world. Icewine is a sweet dessert wine with a sugar level similar to a Sauterne, a Vino Santo or a Tokaji. It is produced predominantly in Ontario's Niagara Peninsula and in the Okanagan Valley of British Columbia. The provinces of Québec, Nova Scotia and New Brunswick produce Icewine in smaller quantities. Canadian Icewines are made from Vidal Blanc, Riesling and Cabernet Franc grapes. Icewines are also made from Gewürztraminer, Chardonnay and Cabernet Sauvignon.

Some U.S. wineries in Northern Michigan use Riesling to make Ice Wine. Note: Icewine is one word in Canada and two words in the United States.

Eiswein is produced in Germany and Austria. Only about five to ten percent of the original crop ends up as Eiswein. In Germany the temperature must be 19°F/-7°C or colder before the grapes can be picked. Grape varieties used include: Sémillon, Sauvignon Blanc, Muscadelle, Riesling, Furmint, Hárslevelű, Muscat, Trebbiano, Malvasia, Pinot Gris and Seyval Blanc.

Icewine, Ice Wine and *Eiswein*, like other dessert wines, are best served with fruity, sweet desserts, ice cream and sorbets. They are also an excellent complement to foie gras, as well as to Roquefort and Stilton cheeses. They are best consumed in five to fifteen years.

Port

Port is a sweet, fortified wine from the Douro region of Portugal, the third oldest protected wine region in the world (1756). Other regions producing Port include Baixo Corgo, Cima Corgo and Douro Superior. Port started to become popular in England between 1703 and 1705 when the English boycotted French wine due to their ongoing political conflicts and began to source red wine from Portugal instead. To ensure that the wine would hold up under the vibration and high temperatures of the ship on its way back to England without spoiling, they "fortified" it by adding a bit of brandy and Port was born. In modern Port production, fortification occurs during fermentation.

Douro Valley

The Douro region forms one of the world's most dramatic vineyard landscapes. In order to provide a flat surface on which to plant the vines on steep hillsides, three landscaping methods are used: traditional stone-walled terraces, *patamares*, meaning platforms and *vinha ao alto*, which means vertical planting.

The Touriga Nacional grape is the mainstay of Port, along with Tinta Roriz (Tempranillo), Touriga Franca, Tinta Cão and Tinta Barroca; Port can be a blend of up to 18 different varieties. These grapes require a dry and continental climate with temperatures reaching up to 110°F/40°C and grow in a soil of schist and granite.

Port comes in a number of different styles. Vintage Port is considered the highest quality of Port and is made only in excellent vintages. In fact, in any given decade only three Vintage Ports may be bottled. Vintage Ports are typically tawny in color and have warm flavors of toffee and chocolate. The wines are slightly viscous and sweet, with coffee or caramel undertones. Late Bottled Vintage (LBV) Port uses less select grapes, but is aged in wood for several years. The wood imparts toasty flavors to the sweet liquid. LBV Port is less expensive than vintage Port and has many similar characteristics.

Non-vintage (NV) Port makes up the majority of Ports. Often Tawny Ports, the blending of juice from multiple vintages leads to consistent flavor. These Ports are warm and sweet with caramel or raisin notes. The aging process of tawny port results in golden colored wines with light sweetness and warm flavors. Ruby Port is a non-vintage Port that is bright red in color. It is aged in both stainless steel vats and in the bottle. It is slightly sweet and often has mild tannins and fruit flavors. White Port is made from multiple vintages of white grapes and is fortified. The wine may be sweet or dry and is relatively mild in flavor. White Port is usually the least expensive.

Port is best when served at around 65°F/18°C. Enjoy Vintage Port with Blue and Stilton cheeses, almonds and walnuts, red grapes and chocolate-based desserts. Ports are on average 20 percent alcohol by volume (ABV). Port is best consumed in 20-50 years.

Port, like any other wine, begins oxidizing as soon as the bottle is opened, which affects its flavor. I would advise finishing a bottle of Port within a week or two of opening it, but it will last up to four weeks after opening if stored properly in the refrigerator. Ruby Port has a slightly longer shelf life than Tawny Port and should be consumed within three to five weeks of opening.

Madeira

Madeira is a fortified white wine that is available in several different styles which vary from dry to sweet. Most Madeira is consumed as an apéritif or as a digestif. Madeira is also used as a flavor agent in cooking. Sercial, Verdelho, Bual and Malmsey are the four principle grape varieties that are used to make the best Madeira wines.

Madeira is unique because it is not only fortified but also oxidized and heated. Madeira is typically amber to dark amber in color with caramel, nut, light spice and wood flavors. Other aroma and flavor notes are vanilla and dried fruits. The alcohol level in Madeira is around 20 percent ABV.

Madeira has several aging classifications: Finest is aged for three years; Reserve for five years; and Special Reserve for 10 years. Extra Reserve is aged for over 15 years, and Vintage bottles are dated for a specific year and aged at least 20 years.

Because it is already oxidized before being bottled, Madeira will remain drinkable for years if properly sealed and stored in the refrigerator. However, just because it will not spoil doesn't mean that it will retain its flavor characteristics and for this reason I would recommend keeping the best quality Madeira for no more than one year.

Cognac and Armagnac

COGNAC

Cognac is named after the town of Cognac (North of Bordeaux) in France. It matures in barrels the same as aged whisky and wine. Maturation in a cask is an essential part of how Cognac is made. It is produced in the regions of Grande Champagne, Petite Champagne, Borderies, Fins Bois, Bons Bois and Bois Communs, and the best grapes are grown in chalky soil. Cognac is made primarily (95 percent) from Ugni Blanc (Trebianno) grapes. The remaining five percent is made from Folle Blanche and Colombard, although the use of Sémillon and Montils grapes is permitted. Depending on the quality and age, Cognac can have flavors of nuts, fruit, caramel, honey, vanilla and various spices. The higher the quality of the Cognac, the smoother it is to drink and the lower the burning sensation. Cognac can be dark caramel, dark amber or mahogany in color, depending on its age. Cognac is usually 40 percent ABV.

Vineyards in Cognac Region

Cognac has several aging qualifications. VS (Very Special) is the lowest tier and is aged for a minimum of two years in casks. VSOP (Very Special Old Pale) is the middle tier, aged for at least four years. XO is the finest grade and is aged for six years or more.

ARMAGNAC

The grapes used to produce Armagnac are split between Ugni Blanc, Folle Blanche, Colombard and Bacco. The color of an Armagnac depends a great deal on how long it has aged. The longer the spirit has spent in wood barrels, the richer the color. Younger Armagnac that hasn't spent much time in wood barrels is golden and honey colored, while older Armagnac is deep brown, deep amber and mahogany in color. A few minutes after the initial scent of alcohol, the aroma and taste are vanilla, wood and roasted nuts with a touch of dried dark fruit. Traditional Armagnac is on average 47 percent ABV. Armagnac's best grapes are grown in sandy soil.

Aging qualifications for Armagnac are as follows. Three Star or VS (Very Special) is a mixture of several Armagnacs that have aged at least two years in wood. VSOP (Very Special Old Pale) is aged in a cask for at least five years. XO is aged at least six years. Older and better Armagnacs are sold as vintages, with the year noted on the label.

TASTE DIFFERENCES

In the grapes, the soil and the process, Armagnac and Cognac are distinctly different products. Armagnac tends to show more fruit than Cognac, in particular orange, plum and apricot. It has notes of vanilla, caramel, toffee, buttered toffee and maple syrup with exotic notes of coconut milk. Armagnacs generally hit their peak between 20 and 30 years of age. Cognac's fruit is of a lighter character, pear and orange, with more floral and spice notes. Cognacs typically peak at around 30 to 40 years.

Sherry

Sherry is produced in Jerez in the Andalusian region of Spain. It is made from the Palomino and Pedro Ximenez grapes and is fortified after fermentation is complete.

There are a number of different types of Sherry, depending on how long they have been aged. The youngest, Fino, is very dry, light-bodied and straw-like in color and has aromas of almonds. Typically, Fino comes in at about 15 percent to 17 percent ABV. It is delicious with olives, almonds, ham, salami and Prosciutto. A "fino style" Sherry, Manzanilla is also dry and pale in color. Amontillado lies somewhere between Fino and Oloroso in terms of color and body. This off-dry Sherry loses its flor (yeast) during the aging process and yields deeper color. Its characteristic flavors and aromas are nutty. Oloroso is dark in color and rich in flavor. Olorosos typically have a remarkable walnut aroma and a soft caramel flavor. Palo Cortado is a very rare Sherry that begins life as a Fino, progresses to an Amontillado and ends up with the richer style of an Oloroso. This Sherry has a dry palate and a lovely reddish-brown color with distinct aromas and full flavor.

Sweet Sherry is a Sherry that has been sweetened with Pedro Ximénez (PX) grape juice. PX grapes have high residual sugar content, as they are sun-dried to concentrate the sugars before being pressed. Flavors from PX are the thick, sweet flavors of fig and molasses.

Cream Sherry is rich mahogany in color and velvety smooth in texture. It is a sweet Sherry made from Amontillado or Oloroso and sweetened with PX. It is excellent with a heavy dessert.

PX is an ultra-sweet, almost syrup-like dessert Sherry, made from sweet, sundried grapes of the same name. Its alcohol content is on the lower end of the spectrum and its flavor profiles are toffee, fig, date and molasses. It, too, is excellent with a heavy dessert.

How long a Sherry lasts after being opened depends on the type of Sherry. Fino or Manzanilla will last for one week in the refrigerator. Amontillado and medium sweet Sherries will last for up to three weeks. Oloroso and Cream Sherries will last four to six weeks and PX will last up to two months.

WHAT FACTORS AFFECT WINE?

Sun, wind, and—of course—soil

From wine what sudden friendship springs!
John Gay

A number of factors affect the taste of wine. The following is a brief overview of each.

Grape Variety

Over centuries, vines have been selected that have key characteristics: pleasant taste, high yields (although this is not always the case), disease resistance and being well-adjusted to the climate in various regions. White wines can be made from either white or red grapes, or a combination of both. The color of the wine is determined by how long the skins remain in the juice.

Soil (*Terroir*)

This refers to the unique combination of natural factors associated with any particular vineyard. They include top soil, subsoil, underlying rock, altitude, slope of hill or terrain, orientation toward the sun, proximity to a body of water and the microclimate. Microclimate elements are rain, winds, humidity and, of course, temperature

Grape Vines in Spring

variation in a given day or season. It is generally agreed that the physical characteristics of soil are the main influence over grapes and thus wine quality. Nutrients and minerals are provided by the soil to help the vines grow. Is the soil chalky, loamy, sandy, volcanic, schist-like, rich in marine fossils, limestone, granite, shale or clay? *Le goût du terroir* (the taste of the soil) is critical to the flavor of wines. Vines, unlike humans, seem to like stress; poor soil often results in better quality grapes.

Climate

Climate means the weather conditions prevailing in an area in general or over a long period of time. Warmth is needed for the production of sugars in grapes. This is why most wines grow between 30° and 50° north and south of the equator.

Sunlight and Exposure

The amount of sunlight the grape vines receive has a dramatic effect on wines. Sunlight allows the grapes to combine CO_2 and water into sugar.

Body of Water

The proximity of a vineyard to a body of water makes a huge difference both in temperature and in the growth of grapes. Germany, Austria and Switzerland are perfect examples of

River Landscape

countries planting along a river, where the sun reflects off the water towards the vineyards.

Slope

In colder climates, vines planted on slopes facing the sun will receive more needed rays. Again, Germany, Austria and Switzerland are excellent examples of countries that plant vines on a slope.

Wine Making

Wines are made from "must", which is a mix, prior to fermentation, of crushed grapes, skins, stems and seeds. Grapes are either black/red or green/white. The pulp of most grapes is white. The color of red and rosé wines comes from the colored skins soaking in the fermenting juice. Rosés are made from red grapes and obtain the pink hue from the skins. The grape skin contact for rosés is between 12 and 36 hours.

Fermentation is the chemical breakdown of the grapes by bacteria, yeasts, or other microorganisms. During fermentation, the sugars in the grapes are converted to alcohol.

Wines can be light, medium or heavy; and dry, semi-dry or sweet.

How the Wine is Matured

Wine can be aged in oak barrels or in stainless steel vats and how the wine is aged affects its taste. Oak barrels can be new or old, French (which gives the wine a softer taste) or American (which gives the wine a more woody taste). Canadian wineries are experimenting with the use of Canadian oak, described as a middle ground between American and French oak. Italian winemakers have a long history of using Slavonian oak, known for its low aromatics and medium level tannins. Croatian barrels are being used more often now because they are less expensive.

If not aged in a barrel, various wood objects can be added to wine as it ages in steel vats in order to introduce the desired taste, for example: oak chips, wood beans or wood shavings (made primarily of oak but also chestnut, pine, redwood or acacia). Every variable in the way the wine is aged is a factor in its final taste.

The Winemaker

Let's talk briefly about what makes our very favorite person great. To start, it helps to have a good nose to smell the bouquet and an exceptional palette to taste the overall flavor of the wine and the unique individual flavor profiles.

Given wine's endless complexity, the winemaker needs a solid knowledge of chemistry and microbiology, if not a degree in either or both fields. It is also most helpful to have a sound understanding of botany, geology, meteorology and entomology.

A graduate degree in winemaking is also a strong start. These programs are offered at schools such as the University of California, Davis. If a degree is not an option, then working as an apprentice at a vineyard is another solid path to becoming a winemaker.

I would submit that the winemaker would need a drop or two of serious common sense to solve problems and work through the less than obvious puzzle of wine making.

Mix all of the above components into a glass of perfectly balanced wine, add a hefty dose of patience and voila! Our best friend, the winemaker, appears.

Two things are certain—no two days at the vineyard are the same, and each day is, to say the least, very interesting.

AT THE TABLE

PART II

WINE ESSENTIALS

*The soft extraction of an aged cork being withdrawn has the true
sound of a man opening his heart.*
William Samuel Benwell

This chapter covers the basics of storing and serving wine. These are not
mere matters of etiquette; how you store and serve your wine has a
profound effect on how you experience it.

Wine Temperature

Please note that when you read "wine is to be served at room temperature"
it does not mean 72°F/22°C. The "room temperature" rule was established
well before air conditioners, radiators and forced hot air. The below
temperatures are key to enjoying a lovely bottle of wine. Being too warm or
too cold will ruin the wine's optimal taste. In general terms, serve red
wines at 52° to 64°F or 11° to 18°C. Serve white wines at 48° to 52°F or 9° to
11°C.

Wine	°F	°C
Barolo, Côtes du Rhône Syrah and Australian Shiraz	64	16 to 18
Aged Bordeaux, Chianti and Rioja	60 to 62	15 to 17
Young Burgundy, Pinot Noir, Bordeaux, Chianti, Zinfandel, Rioja	56 to 59	13 to 16
Beaujolais and Valpolicella	52	10 to 11
Sherry, Madeira and Port	50	10
Riesling, Sauvignon Blanc, Gewürztraminer and Pinot Grigio	45 to 50	8 to 10
Chardonnay, Grüner Veltliner, Viognier	55 to 58	12 to 14
Rosé	48 to 52	9 to 11
Champagne	44 to 46	7 to 8
Sweet white wine	42	6

Wine Storage Conditions

Red wines should be stored at 52° to 60° F or 10° to 14°C. White wines should be stored at around 45° to 50° F or 6° to 9°C. Wines should be kept away from sunlight and heat exposure. It is best to store them in a wine cellar, a wine refrigerator or a temperature-controlled cool room. Wide fluctuations in temperature will damage both the wine and the cork.

Wine Glasses

It is difficult to enjoy a good wine in a bad glass.
Evelyn Waugh

The glass you drink from is very important in that it very much affects the wine's bouquet, so appropriate glasses should be used as much as possible.

Look for glasses that have a long stem to allow for a comfortable grip and a base that is large enough to be steady. The advantages of holding the stem are to avoid marking the glass and to prevent the warming of the wine in its bowl.

Fill the bowl of the glass 1//3 to 1/2 full, depending on the size of the glass. Space is needed to fully enjoy the bouquet.

Serve sparkling wines in fluted glasses to allow the bubbles to pearl upwards.

Alsace has its own glasses for Rieslings. They are tall and green-stemmed.

If you are interested in tasting wines correctly, then you may want to have glasses that are neither colored nor cut. The idea is to drink from clear, uncut glass to better read the wine. Also, it is best for a wine tasting to have wine glasses with stems. This keeps one from warming the bowl and thus the wine, and allows the bowl to stay clear in order to better study the color and hues of the wine.

The Corkscrew

I prefer the basic waiter's key, which has a small knife to cut the capsule/collar/foil. Its two-tiered hinge prevents cork breakage, especially when pulling the long corks found in fine wines. And it has a fine and tightly-wound spiral made of silicone that is two-and-a-half inches long.

The Cork

Corks are made from the bark of an oak tree known as the Corkwood. The outer bark can be safely stripped away every nine or so years from a mature tree that is approximately 15 to 25 years old. Corkwoods are mainly grown and harvested in Portugal and Spain. Some wineries use alternative corks from composite plastics to avoid corkage (the wine spoiling in the bottle) and New World countries such as Australia, New Zealand, the United States and Canada are popularizing twist tops as well. Even Old World countries are starting to use twist tops. Why is this so important to the wine trade? It has been calculated that between five to nine percent of all wines are corked upon arrival to their destination, which is unaffordable.

A Corkwood Tree

When to Drink Wine

Unless it is a high-end collectible, like my 1961 Chateaux Lafitte-Rothschild from Bordeaux, drink away. Too many folks hold wines until they lose their peak flavor and it is a shame. Generally, wines, especially whites, last one to two years before they start to deteriorate. When a white wine has darkened over time, it has maderized. As a result, it acquires a Sherry-like character, which is not at all desirable with white wines.

Keeping Wine in Open Bottles Fresh

The time frames vary depending on the specific type of wine, but for still whites, reds and rosés, two to three days is the absolute maximum amount of time that I recommend keeping an opened bottle to consume. After that point, any remaining wine can be used for cooking for two to three weeks. But before using it to cook, smell or taste the wine to make sure that it has not gone off (taken on a vinegar-like character).

Champagne, Prosecco or other sparkling wines are pretty much dead after they've been opened, since the carbonation dissolves very quickly when the wine is exposed to oxygen.

The very best way to extend the life of an opened bottle is to keep it in the refrigerator and to plug it with its original cork, but I prefer a tight-fitting bottle stopper along with a pump system that can be found in any wine shop. The pump with two plugs usually sells for about $15. There is also a system that allows you to inject a kind of inert gas into the bottle to replace the air. You can acquire a simple canister of inert gas for around $10. Both systems are quite good, but please remember that a good bottle of wine should be finished when it is opened, as some of the fruity notes, its aroma, its body and just about everything else, including the delicate nuances, will be lost. This holds true for all wine types. A wine will deteriorate much more quickly if left on your countertop at room temperature.

Decanting

When should you decant? The general reason for decanting is to separate any sediment from the clear wine. You will usually find sediment in older bottles that were stored on their sides. The other reason to decant is to aerate the wine; to allow it to breathe. If I have a special bottle and want it to aerate more quickly to improve its qualities, then I decant it. It is best to decant at the table just before your special meal, as you do not want an older wine to be exposed to air for too long a period. Remember to leave the empty bottle on the table after decanting so that your guests can read and enjoy the label.

HOW TO DECANT

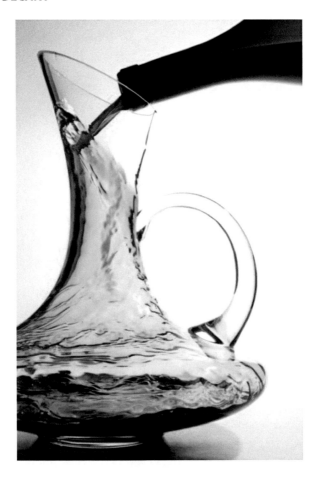

Decanting is actually a very simple process. You need a clean and dry glass container. You may wish to use a candle to ensure you see exactly when the sediment is at the neck of the bottle. Gently and very slowly pour the wine into the decanter. When you see the light sediment in the neck of the bottle, stop pouring. Enjoy!

Serving Order

When serving more than one wine, the order in which they are served is crucial, as you do not want heavier flavors to overpower lighter ones. Follow these general rules:

- Serve dry wine before sweet wine.
- Serve light-bodied wine before full-bodied wine.
- Serve white wine before red wine.
- Serve old wine before young wine.

WINE ETIQUETTE

Wine makes every meal an occasion, every table more elegant, every day more civilized.
Andre Simon

When cutting the capsule (also known as the collar or the foil), cut below the *second* tier or flange. This practice originated because foils were historically made of lead, and research has shown that trace amounts of toxic lead could remain on the lip of the bottle and mix with the poured wine. Today foils are made of tin or aluminum.

Never remove the foil in its entirety. The capsule dresses the neck of the bottle and looks far better for presentation purposes.

The host or the person who brought the bottle as a gift should always taste the wine before serving to the other people at the table.

Never "wound" (or scar) the front label (*ne blessez jamais l'étiquette*); that is, do not allow wine to touch the front label after pouring. The best way to avoid this is by protecting the front label with the palm of the hand you are pouring with.

To avoid staining the table while pouring, use a small napkin to wipe the bottle's neck after each pour. Small inserts for pouring are also available, but check first over the sink to ensure they are working correctly.

Do not touch the edge of a wine glass with the neck of the bottle when pouring as you might chip the glass.

Ice in wine is considered a "sin". It dilutes the flavor of the wine.

Glasses are placed to the right and wine is served to the person's right. Note, in the image below, there is a water goblet, a red wine glass and a white wine glass. White wine glasses are usually smaller than red wine glasses. The water goblet is usually the largest glass of the three.

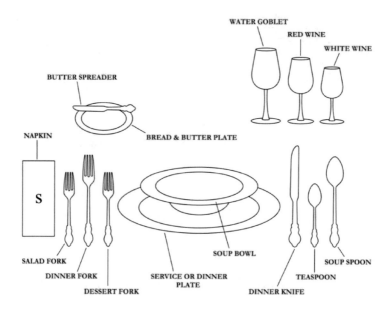

HOW TO TASTE WINE

Wine...offers a greater range for enjoyment and appreciation than possibly any other purely sensory thing which may be purchased.
Ernest Hemingway

The last thing you want when uncorking a bottle of wine is to serve a bad drop to your friends at home or your guests at dinner in a restaurant. For that reason alone, it is imperative to observe, sniff, swirl, sniff again and taste. In general only sniff red corks to ensure the wine is clean and hasn't gone bad, that is, to make sure it is not "corked". First, look at the wine when it is still in the glass to observe its appearance. Sniff before swirling to gauge the first notes. Swirl the wine in the glass to get the molecules working and the aroma more vibrant. Sniff again and then taste a little. Have the wine travel in your whole mouth, hitting your tongue, upper and lower gums and cheeks. If you wish, when tasting the wine, you may draw in a little air to accentuate the flavor. If at this point it tastes fine to you, then pour away. Enjoy!

DESCRIBING WINE

To enjoy wine ... what is needed is a sense of smell, a sense of taste,
an eye for color. All else is experience and personal preference.
Cyril Ray

Too many people get intimidated with regards to the descriptions we use when tasting wine. Here is the number ONE rule: Enjoy yourself and the wine. Below are some of the key wine terms used when tasting and/or critiquing wine.

Appearance (Sight)

Describe the intensity of the wine's color as being pale, medium or deep/dark. Describe its clarity as being clear or dull/opaque/flat. Describe the color as:

- White wines: lemon, gold, amber
- Rosé wines: purple, salmon, orange
- Red wines: purple, ruby, garnet/brick, tawny (This is the spectrum of color as red wines age.)

Nose (Smell)

To describe the intensity of the wine's nose, are the flavor notes light, medium or pronounced? Does it smell "clean" or "dull"? Clean means fresh and clear to the nose and free of any off-odor, while dull means lacking in distinct varietal character. To describe the wine's aroma, refer to flavor characteristics below.

Palate (Taste)

Describe a wine's sweetness as sweet, off-dry (slightly sweet), or dry (not sweet). Describe acidity as low, medium or high. Describe tannin (usually for reds) as low, medium or high. Is the wine's body full or thin? To determine the wine's length, do the feel and flavor stay in the mouth after swallowing for a short or for a long time?

Basic Flavor Characteristics

WHITE WINES

Flavor characteristics for white wines are citrus, green fruit, tropical fruit, floral, spice (think Gewürztraminer), mineral/steel and butter.

ROSÉ WINES

Flavor characteristics for rosé wines are more subtle notes of strawberry, cherry and raspberry with some citrus and watermelon.

RED WINES

Red wines can have red fruit, black fruit (such as raspberry, strawberry and blackberry), dried fruit, cooked jam (stewed fruits), chocolate, spice, leather, oak, or vanilla flavors.

SPARKLING WINES

Sparkling wines have citrus, green fruit, tropical fruit, floral, yeast, bread, or toast flavors.

FOOD AND WINE PAIRING:
IT'S ALL IN THE SAUCE

The primary purpose of wine is to make food taste better.
Myra Waldo

The net of it is that light foods call for light wines, robust foods call for big wines and the sauce dictates the pairing. Remember one other key point: seasoning also determines the pairing. Let me give an example. Chicken with a strong tarragon sauce would defer to the sauce when choosing the wine, as the spice outweighs the flavor of the meat. See Key Rules on page 58.

Food Flavors

SALTY

Oysters and other shellfish call for crisp, dry whites such as Muscadet and Chablis. Sancerre from the Loire Valley and Sauvignon Blanc from other regions also go well with oysters and shellfish.

SWEET

Sweet wines such as Sauternes, ice wines and Beaumes-de-Venise should be sweeter than the dessert otherwise they will seem thin.

SOUR

Here you are looking for wine with a good level of acidity: Sauvignon Blanc, Riesling or a light red such as Valpolicella.

SAVORY

An example of a savory dish is Rizotto and mushrooms. Choose medium to full reds. Avoid whites as the flavors of savory will overpower them.

SMOKY

Pair smoked salmon with Riesling. With BBQ meats, pair a Shiraz or Zinfandel/Primitivo.

SPICY

Consider wines that are unoaked, ripe and fruity such as dry Rieslings, which are the best match by far for spicy food. Other good choices are Gewürztraminer, Grüner Veltliner, Sémillon and Viognier grape varieties.

Foods

BEEF/STEAK

Serve reds, including Cabernet Sauvignon, heavier Merlots, Grenache, Nebbiolo, Malbec, Syrah, Tannat and heavy Portuguese reds.

VEAL/PORK

Pair with Chardonnay, Chenin Blanc, Sauvignon Blanc, Grüner Veltliner, Beaujolais, Merlot, Cabernet Franc, Syrah or Côtes du Rhône (Grenache).

HAM

Enjoy a Chablis, unoaked Chardonnay, Grüner Veltliner, Merlot, Pinot Noir, Cabernet Franc or Beaujolais.

LAMB

Serve Bordeaux blends, Spanish Rioja or Ribera del Duero, Malbec, Xynomavro, Nebbiolo, Syrah or Grenache.

CHICKEN

Pair with Chardonnay, Grüner Veltliner, Chenin Blanc, Sémillon, a light Sauvignon Blanc, Pinot Noir, Cabernet Franc or Gamay.

TURKEY

Serve Champagne, Riesling, Sémillon, Gewürztraminer, Grüner Veltliner; and for reds Zinfandel, a well-structured Pinot Noir, Gamay, Cabernet Franc or perhaps a Beaujolais Nouveau.

DUCK

Serve Sémillon, Riesling, Merlot, Malbec, Grenache, Cabernet Franc or a heavier Pinot Noir.

LIGHT FISH

With light fish such as trout and Salmon serve Chardonnay, but not too oaky as the notes of vanilla, wood and caramel will overpower the delicate flavors of the light fish. Consider also a Pinot Gris/Pinot Grigio or a light Pinot Noir.

FISH STEAKS

With fish steaks such as tuna, shark or swordfish, serve Sauvignon Blanc, Chenin Blanc, unoaked Chardonnay, Merlot, Pinot Noir, Tempranillo or Cabernet Franc.

SHELLFISH

Serve Muscadet, Chablis, Sauvignon Blanc, Viognier, Grüner Veltliner or Sancerre.

PATÉ

Serve Beaujolais, but not Beaujolais Nouveau, because it is too fruity and too light in tannin and cannot stand up to the paté. You may wish to also try a Chenin Blanc.

CHEESES

With Camembert and Brie serve Merlot, Pinot Noir, or Valpolicella. With hard cheeses such as Cheddar serve a heavier Chardonnay, Rioja, right bank Bordeaux with more Merlot, Grenache, or Gamay. With blue cheeses, classic pairings include Roquefort cheese with Sauternes and Stilton cheese with Port. Why not try a Canadian Icewine or a Hungarian Tokaji?

PASTA

Clearly "it's all in the sauce" is key here, but as a general rule go with Italian wines, as there are so many wonderful choices: a good Chianti, Frascati, Valpolicella, Soave, Gavi, Barbera, Montepulciano d'Abruzzo, Negroamaro, Barolo, Barbaresco, Brunello di Montalcino or Amarone for special occasions.

SMOKED SALMON

A nice brut Champagne is the very best, but please consider Sancerre, Pouilly-Fumé and Muscadet. Other nice matches are Chablis, a dry Riesling from Alsace and Gavi from Italy. If you prefer reds then consider a light and fruity Beaujolais or a Pinot Noir.

ASIAN FLAVORS

Serve with Muscadet, Sauvignon Blanc, Sémillon, Chenin Blanc, Verdelho, a fruity rosé, Zinfandel or a Beaujolais.

SPICY ASIAN

Pair with Riesling, Pinot Gris, Gewürztraminer, Shiraz, Viognier, Sémillon or Grüner Veltliner.

INDIAN

Serve with Sémillon, Chardonnay, Pinotage, Shiraz or a Shiraz blend.

Key Rules for Pairing Wine with Food

Follow these simple rules for pairing wine with food and you shouldn't go wrong.

1. Look for compatible weights and bodies. The essence of this rule embodies the age old "red wine with red meat, white wine with fish and white meat", although this is more of a suggestion than a rule. Just ensure that the weight and body of the dish is consistent with the weight and body of the wine.

2. Look for compatible acidity levels. When pairing food with wine, make sure that the acidity level in both are about the same. A good example is a dish like lemon chicken paired with a high acid Vernaccia from Italy.

3. Look for complementary flavors and complexities. Food and wine shouldn't fight one another for your attention. Instead, they should achieve synergy, complementing each other's best traits. A complex, elegant meal deserves a complex wine, whereas the flavors of a simple meal could be lost in the same.

4. When serving a food with a pronounced sauce, pair the wine to the flavors in the sauce. The same applies to seasoning: a delicate Pinot Noir would be overwhelmed by an Indian Curry, whereas a Zinfandel would overpower a delicate lemon butter sauce on your trout.

5. When matching wine to a food without a pronounced sauce or seasoning, pair to the flavors in the main ingredient instead of to the strongest flavor. Beef and roasted or grilled meats will withstand a heavier wine but will wipe out all flavor of a more sensitive one.

Wine Killers

The following, for the most part, can kill the flavor of wines, so try to stay away from these, especially if you have a very special wine that you plan to present "on center stage".

Be wary of anchovies, raw mushrooms, artichokes, garlic, tomatoes and asparagus, and especially vinaigrettes with a high concentration of vinegar.

Green Artichokes

THE LABEL

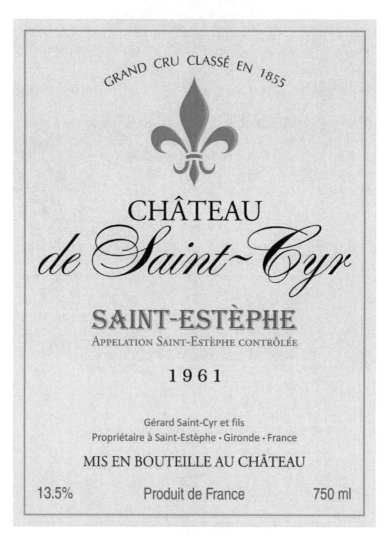

GRAND CRU CLASSÉ EN 1855

CHÂTEAU
de Saint-Cyr

SAINT-ESTÈPHE
APPELATION SAINT-ESTÈPHE CONTRÔLÉE

1961

Gérard Saint-Cyr et fils
Propriétaire à Saint-Estèphe · Gironde · France

MIS EN BOUTEILLE AU CHÂTEAU

13.5%   Produit de France   750 ml

For Purposes of Illustration Only

Montrachet should be drunk kneeling with one's head bared.
Alexandre Dumas

The Typical Wine Label

FAIR HAVEN VINEYARD
OLD VINE ZINFANDEL
NAPA VALLEY, CALIFORNIA

1992

750 ml   ALC. 15.0 % BY VOL.

For Purposes of Illustration Only

Above is an example of an American label. On the previous page is an example of a French label. The following sections explain the different pieces of information that you find on the typical wine label.

WINERY OR PRODUCER'S NAME

Who made the wine? This is the most important piece of information on the label. In essence it is the author of the wine.

GRAPE VARIETY/VARIETIES

In the New World, grape varieties are clearly stated. In the Old World, a geographical appellation is the key. Burgundy whites are made from Chardonnay while the reds are, with few exceptions, Pinot Noir.

COUNTRY AND REGION

The label tells you where the grapes in the wine were grown. It can be a general region (e.g., Napa Valley), or a very specific one (e.g., a Domaine in Burgundy). The more specific the appellation, the finer the wine.

VINTAGE

How old is the wine? The date tells you when the grapes were harvested. The vintage is important to collectors because a year's unique weather will affect the harvest, the flavor profile of a wine and its monetary value.

ALCOHOL CONTENT

Alcohol content means the level of alcohol in percentage by volume. Note that in the United States the law permits a 1.5 percent spread, so if the label states 13 percent it may be 11.5 percent to 14.5 percent.

LEGAL ADVISORY

The words "Contains Sulfites" must be included by law. Because of the use of sulfur dioxide in the making of wines, all wines have some level of sulfites by the end of the process.

BACK LABEL

It seems that New World wines use the back label to sell their wines. They often include the history, geographic location, including proximity to a body of water or its altitude, a description of the vineyard's landscape, percentage of each grape variety, flavor profiles and food-pairing recommendations. On occasion, the marketing team from a New World vineyard will even throw in some humor.

The back labels of Old World wines are more serious. I have a red Bordeaux in my hand and the back label tells us the following: The château, the region, the vintage, shipped by, imported by, alcohol level, net contents, government warning, country of origin and "contains sulfites".

Decoding the German Wine Label

For Purposes of Illustration Only

There are eleven items of information on the above German wine label, not including the alcohol level and the quality of the wine, which would add up to thirteen. Clearly thirteen is quite the number and German labels are, without a doubt, the most confusing in the wine world. Let's attempt to make this simple.

GRAPE VARIETY

If one grape variety makes up 75 percent or more of the wine it is listed on the label. If the percentage is less than 75 percent then the wine listed, by law, is Riesling.

VINTAGE

If 85 percent of the grapes come from one year the vintage is permitted to be listed. It is often followed by the suffix "-er".

REGION

There are 13 wine regions in Germany. See page 138.

VILLAGE/VINEYARD

This is a two-word statement. The first word is the village and the second word denotes a single vineyard or a group of vineyards.

QUALITY CLASSIFICATION

There are five quality levels for German wines. They are listed below from the highest to the lowest quality:

1. *Qualitätswein mit Prädikat* (QmP): Quality Wine with Distinction is the top tier.

2. *Qualitätswein bestimmten Anbaugebietes* (QbA): Quality Wine from a Specific Region is Germany's second tier of wine quality classification.

3. *Qualitätswein* (Q): Quality Wine.

4. *Landwein* (L): Country Wine or Wine from the Land.

5. *Tafelwein* (T): Table Wine is the lowest level. A percentage of the grapes can come from other countries. If 50 percent or more of the grapes come from Germany, it is usually labeled *Deutscher Tafelwein* (DT) which means German Table Wine.

PRÄDIKAT LEVEL (QMP)

The Prädikat level (QmP), of which there are six, determines the ripeness of the grapes at harvest and the alcohol level:

1. *Kabinett*: Literally "cabinet," which is where German hosts used to keep the good bottle to bring out for guests with dinner. The lightest wine, dry or off-dry.

2. *Spätlese*: "Late harvest". Usually fuller-bodied and off-dry, but can be dry.

3. *Auslese*: "Selected late harvest". The ripest bunches are selected by the harvesters in repeated trips through the vineyard. Medium-sweet.

4. *Beerenauslese (BA)*: "Selected berries; late harvest". The ripest individual grapes are selected in repeated trips through the vineyard.
5. *Eiswein*: "Ice wine". Eiswein has a similar ripeness level as *Beerenauslese*. The grapes freeze on the vine before picking. They are both quite sweet, intense dessert wines. See page 30.

6. There is also *Trockenbeerenauslese (TBA)*: "Individual dried berries, selected late harvest". In this case, the grapes hang so long that they dry up on the vine a little, like wet raisins. They have to be pressed to get any juice, and it takes about 20,000 grapes to make a bottle of wine. Both *Beerenauslese* and *TBA* are almost always affected by Botrytis Cinerea, the same Noble Rot of Sauternes. TBA is a very sweet and very concentrated wine.

For more information on the QmP, you may wish to study the pyramid on page 141.

PRODUCER

This is the name of the winemaker.

ADDRESS

This is the address where the wine was bottled. If the wine was bottled at the winery, then the address is for both the winery and the bottling location.

BOTTLING STATEMENT

You will find one of the following:

1. *Aus dem Lesegut.* Bottled by the producer. The grapes may be grown by two or more producers. This statement is generally used by the *négociants* (see page 96).

2. *Erzeugerabfüllung.* Grown, produced and bottled by the estate.

3. *Erzeugergemeinschaft.* Produced and bottled by a Co-op.

4. *Gutsabfüllung.* Single estate grown, produced and bottled.

5. *Schlossabfüllung.* Château bottled.

AP NUMBER

AP stands for *Amtliche Prufungsnummer* which is found on all Q, QbA and QmP labels. It is a quality control number code indicating the testing station, vineyard code, bottler code and finally the bottling year.

THE SPECIAL EAGLE SYMBOL

The special eagle symbol is permitted to be used only by the top 200 producers in Germany and they are voted by the producers themselves, not the government. VDP stands for *Verband Deutscher Pradikatsweinguter* which is the Association of German Predicates. See eagle symbol on page 63.

WINE

REGIONS

OF THE

WORLD

PART III

WINE REGIONS OF THE WORLD

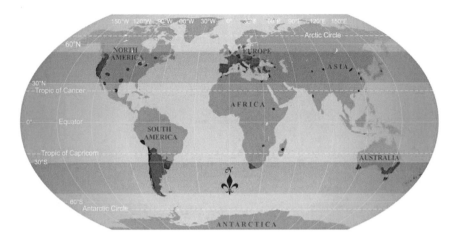

This is one of the disadvantages of wine, it makes a man mistake words for thoughts.
Samuel Johnson

Sixty-six countries produced over 27 billion liters of wine in 2014, and in this part of the book we embark on a wine tour of 17 of them. The following chapters cover the major wine-producing countries that import the most wine into the United States and Canada.

A country is distinguished by its wines, as much as it is by its landscape, cultures and languages. We will visit each region and get a close-up look of what is growing where. We'll stop to soak up the climate in each area and sift its regions' soil between our fingertips. In each country, we'll learn a little about the history of wine-making; the processes used to certify wines; what kinds of wines are produced and how each country ranks in world wine production. Along the way, I will also share some of my personal experiences touring vineyards, tasting wines and harvesting grapes.

THE UNITED STATES

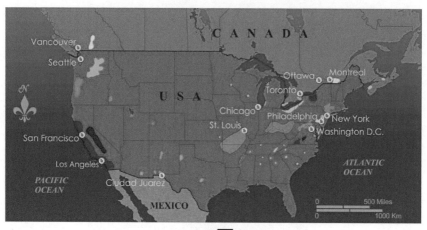

Map of U.S. and Canada Wine Regions

French Huguenot settlers made the United States' first wine from the Scuppernong (Muscadine) grape variety at a Florida settlement in the 1560s, and wines have been produced in the United States for over 300 years. Today it is the fourth largest wine-producing country in the world, with over 8,000 wineries scattered throughout the 50 states.

Consumer interest in wines is increasing, and the U.S. wine industry grows about seven percent to eight percent annually. Beer consumption grows approximately two percent to three percent per year, while hard alcohol consumption falls about five percent to six percent per year.

Today wines are produced in all U.S. states, though only four of them account for 97 percent of all wines produced, namely California (about 90 percent), New York (around 3.3 percent), Washington (close to 3.3 percent) and Oregon (approximately one percent).

The United States uses the term American Viticultural Area (AVA) on its wine labels. An AVA is a designated region in the United States where grapes are grown for wine. An AVA is distinguishable by geographic features, and its boundaries are defined by the Alcohol and Tobacco Tax and Trade Bureau (TTB), which falls under the United States Department of the Treasury. The AVA system is similar to (but not quite as precise as) the French AOP system (see page 97). A wine using an AVA designation must originate from within the boundaries of the AVA, and at least 85 percent of the grapes used in the wine must come from the AVA area. If a

70

year appears on the label, at least 95 percent of the grapes in the wine must be from that particular vintage. A vineyard may be located in more than one AVA, for example, when a smaller AVA is located within a larger (regional) AVA.

California

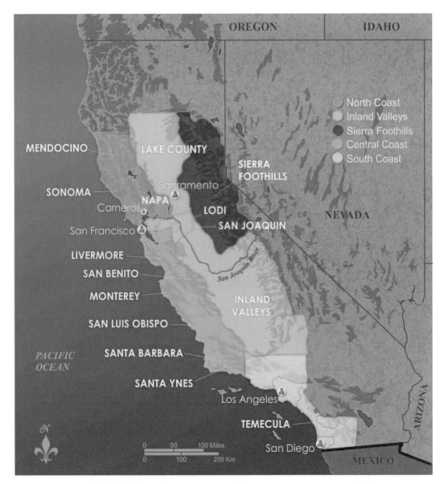

California accounts for nearly 90 percent of American wine production and it is the fourth leading wine-producing region in the world, behind France, Italy and Spain. The state's viticultural history dates back to the 18th century, when Spanish missionaries planted the first vineyards with each mission they established. Wine was used for religious sacraments as well as for daily life. Today there are more than 4,000 wineries and over 5,000 vineyards in California. According to the Wine Institute of California, there are currently 134 AVAs in the state. If an AVA is to be used on the label, at least 85 percent of the grapes must come from the defined area. (To use a county name on a Californian wine label, at least 75 percent of the grapes must come from that county). The top red grapes produced are Cabernet Sauvignon, Zinfandel, Merlot, Rubired (Tintoria), Pinot Noir and Syrah; and the top whites are Chardonnay, French Colombard, Pinot Gris, Sauvignon Blanc and Muscat.

California has over 570,000 acres (525,000 bearing fruit) of planted vines mostly located in a stretch of land covering over 700 miles (1,100 km) from Mendocino County to the southwestern tip of Riverside County and hundreds of micro-climates. Its 134 AVAs include the well-known Napa Valley, Russian River Valley, Rutherford, Sonoma County and Paso Robles. The Inland Valleys are California's largest wine region stretching for 300 miles (480 km) from the Sacramento Valley south to the San Joaquin Valley. The Inland Valleys produce nearly 70 percent of all the grape crush that is used to make California's bulk, box and jug wine. Chardonnay is the most widely planted wine grape, followed by Cabernet Sauvignon. California's five regions and its most prominent AVAs are discussed below. Soil throughout California is sand, clay, loam, granite, volcanic ash, seabed soil and river-run gravel.

In August 2012, I finally made it to the American Mecca of wines: The Napa and Sonoma Valleys. The beauty of the region was breathtaking, and the newness surprised me compared to the historical cellars I had visited so many times in Europe.

What impressed me so much was the sunny weather, the hilly landscape and the perfectly manicured vineyards. The full-bodied Cabernet Sauvignon, Merlot and Zinfandel wines were all fruit forward with high alcohol content and were splendidly balanced. The Chardonnay wines I tasted at a number of vineyards

Multi-colored Grapes

were refreshing, crisp and so natural in flavor. I must say that all of the food met my high expectations as well. As you can imagine, just as with

France, Italy and Spain, a book could easily be written about the California wine regions alone; but below I highlight only the best known.

NORTH COAST

California's most well-known wine regions are Napa Valley and Sonoma Valley, as well as the adjacent regions of Mendocino and Lake Counties.

Napa Valley

The Napa Valley wine region is located 50 miles north of San Francisco, California. It is bordered by the Vaca mountain range on the east and the Myacamas on the west; by Mt. St. Helena at the north and by the San Pablo Bay at the south. It is the most densely concentrated wine region in the world, with over 600 wineries producing some of the very best Chardonnay, Cabernet Sauvignon and Merlot wines. One of my favorite wines is Joseph Phelps Insignia from St. Helena, which I would recommend for a special occasion. The area's Mediterranean climate (warm, sunny days followed by cool evenings) and the skill of its

Vineyard with Autumn Colors

winemakers contribute to its popularity. In most parts, Napa Valley is only a few miles wide with low volcanic hills and soils of volcanic and alluvial origin.

The Napa Valley was established as an AVA in 1981. There are 16 AVAs within the Napa Valley AVA, each with distinct microclimates and terrains as a result of their various configurations of hills, exposures and elevations. Napa crushes about four percent of California's total wine tonnage.

Sonoma County

Sonoma County is located above San Francisco between the northern California coast and Napa Valley along the Mayacamas Range. Mendocino County lies to the north and Marin County to the south. The wine industry in Sonoma is generally on a smaller scale than that of the Napa wine region, though it does contain over 800 wineries and 16 distinct AVAs.

Chardonnay is the most planted grape variety, Cabernet Sauvignon is the second followed by Pinot Noir. Sonoma County produces about six percent of California's total wine.

The climate here is cooler than that of Napa Valley and varies dramatically depending on the appellation, making Sonoma County an ideal location for growing grapes. Ocean-side vineyards are cooled by offshore breezes and fogs. Microclimates are influenced by the Russian River and the Pacific Ocean. The soil is volcanic.

Mendocino County

Located directly north of Sonoma County and about 90 miles north of San Francisco, the mountainous Mendocino wine region, which includes Lake County, is bounded by California's Coastal Mountain Range, the Pacific Ocean and the great northern redwood forests. Most vineyards are located in the inland valleys to the south and to the east. White wine grape varieties are located on flood plains and alluvium along the Navarro and Russian Rivers. Most of the red varieties are grown on the bench lands above.

Of the 10 distinct winegrowing regions within Mendocino County, eight are official AVAs, and the remaining two are proposed viticultural areas. There are approximately 100 wineries and over 250 growers harvesting about two percent of the state's wine tonnage. Across 17,000 acres of vineyards, the top grape varieties cultivated are Chardonnay, Cabernet Sauvignon, Pinot Noir, Sauvignon Blanc, Zinfandel and Gewürztraminer.

CENTRAL COAST

Monterey County

The Monterey wine-growing region, with 43,000 acres of planted grape vines, is located below San Francisco on the central California coast and contains around 60 wineries. San Bernabe, the world's largest contiguous vineyard (over 8,700 acres), is also located in the area.

Chardonnay is the most important variety here, comprising 43 percent of the total grape acreage. Monterey is the number one producer of Pinot Noir with 22 percent of the California crop. There are also roughly 2,800 acres of wine grapes planted in San Benito County and eight wineries. Together, San Benito and Monterey counties account for about eight percent of the state's wine production.

The climate of Monterey County reflects the cooling influence of the Monterey Bay and lack of abundant rainfall. There are a sufficient number of warm days to ripen the grapes, however the marine influence predominates. Due to the cool growing conditions, harvest is typically two weeks later than other California regions, allowing for a long season and slow fruit maturation. The steep slopes provide good drainage, and Monterey soil temperatures are cooler than other parts of the state, limiting crop size. Due to the cool climate, grapes such as Merlot, Riesling and Chenin Blanc also do very well here.

Santa Barbara County

The Santa Barbara wine-growing region is located above Los Angeles on the central California coast. In Santa Barbara County, the north-south coastal range of mountains turns to run almost east-west for 50 miles, framing the valleys in a unique transit to the Pacific Ocean. The unique topography allows the flow of fog and ocean breezes

California Vineyards

to shape distinct microclimates and makes the region one of the coolest viticultural areas in California, though warmer daytime temperatures in the inland areas allow a wide variety of grapes to be grown. Terrain and climates vary widely, from steep, wind-swept hillsides to rolling inland valley vineyards where summer temperatures often reach the century mark. There are 21,000 vineyard acres planted in Santa Barbara County growing over 55 varieties of grapes, with more than 175 wineries.

The five AVAs are Santa Rita Hills, Santa Maria Valley, Happy Canyon, Ballard Canyon and Santa Ynez Valley. The unique soil and the maritime influence in this region, which is becoming renowned for its cool climate and ideal growing conditions, are perfect for producing Pinot Noir, Chardonnay, Cabernet Sauvignon, Sauvignon Blanc, Riesling and Syrah.

Paso Robles

Paso Robles is located halfway between San Francisco and Los Angeles on the central California coast, in San Luis Obispo County. There are 32,000 acres of wine grapes planted within Paso Robles and 11 AVAs. The number one wine grape variety here is Cabernet Sauvignon. Merlot is second, followed by Chardonnay. There are about 200 wineries in Paso Robles.

The city of Paso Robles is California's fastest-growing wine region and largest geographic appellation. It has the greatest day-to-night temperature fluctuation of any Californian appellation. Days are warm and clear and the area is generally free of clouds, fog or severe winds. Nighttime temperatures are about 40°F/4.4°C cooler, due to the area's proximity to the ocean. This, along with geographic configurations and varying elevations, means diverse microclimates, allowing production of both cool and warm climate grape varieties. Soil is granite, shale and sandstone.

More than 40 wine grape varieties are grown in Paso Robles to produce high end wines. 80 percent of the grapes grown here are reds; Cabernet Sauvignon, Merlot, Syrah and Zinfandel, the area's heritage wine variety. Whites include Chardonnay, Viognier and Roussanne.

INLAND VALLEYS (SACRAMENTO AND SAN JOAQUIN)

East of the San Francisco Bay and running south through the Sacramento and San Joaquin valleys to Bakersfield, lie the Inland Valleys. Its eight AVAs are as follows: Clarksburg, Diablo Grande, Dunnigan Hills, Lodi, Madera, Merritt Island, River Junction and Salado Creek. The Sierra Foothills AVA runs along the east side of both valleys, adjacent to the Sierra Nevada Mountains. Viticulture here actually takes place in two valleys; the Sacramento Valley (8,000 acres) and the San Joaquin Valley (151,000 acres); and in the delta where the two valleys meet (100,000 acres). Chardonnay is the most widely planted variety and Zinfandel is a close second. The Delta accounts for over 20 percent of the total state grape crush. Neither Sacramento Valley nor the San Joaquin Valley are themselves AVAs, but more than 70 percent of California's grapes are produced in the Inland Valleys.

Within the Delta area, the Lodi AVA has been a significant wine-growing region since the 1850s. Today it is cultivated by over 750 growers and is home to approximately 85 wineries. Delta wine areas are influenced by their proximity to the Pacific Ocean and by the coastal gap where the northern and southern coastal ranges meet at the San Francisco Bay. When temperatures rise in the vast Inland Valleys, cool breezes from the Pacific are pulled across the Delta, creating a unique Mediterranean microclimate that, along with deep, sandy clay loam soils, has produced premium wine grapes for over a hundred years.

Sunny, rich-soiled and not subject to any ocean influences, the Sacramento Valley is home to 16 wineries and approximately 8,000 acres of wine grapes; predominantly Chardonnay, but with Zinfandel running a close second. The San Joaquin Valley, home to over 45 wineries and a total of 152,000 acres of wine grapes, is one of the most fertile agricultural areas in the world, and most of the wine, table and raisin grapes grown in California are grown here in this valley. French Colombard is the predominantly-grown white variety, followed by Chardonnay. The red grape with the most acreage is Zinfandel followed by Cabernet Sauvignon. Over 45 percent of California's total wine grape crush is grown here, making the San Joaquin Valley the top producing area in the state.

Though rainfall is limited, Grapes have been grown here for over a century and two massive reservoir and canal systems are used for irrigation. New grape varieties, rootstocks, trellis systems and advancements in irrigation techniques are transforming the San Joaquin Valley from a generic producer to a producer of varietal wines.

SIERRA FOOTHILLS

Wine grapes were first planted in the Sierra Foothills in 1849 during the California Gold Rush. The Sierra Foothills AVA, along the western edge of the Sierra Nevada, was established in 1987. It is roughly 160 miles long, totals 5,700 vineyard acres and includes five other AVAs: California's Shenandoah Valley, El Dorado, Fair Play, Fiddletown and North Yuba. Zinfandel is most predominantly planted, followed by Cabernet Sauvignon, Syrah, Chardonnay, Merlot and Barbera. Over one hundred wineries can be found tucked into the nooks and crannies of the foothills; vineyards are generally located at between 1,500 ft (460 m) to 3,000 ft (915 m), where the elevation creates a four-season climate. The soil is granite.

SOUTH COAST

In 1769 the first wine grapes in California were planted by a Franciscan missionary at Mission San Diego de Alcala. The oldest winery in California, Mission San Gabriel near LA, was established in 1771. In California's smallest wine region, proximity to the Pacific Ocean, micro-climates and rich soils produce quality Chardonnay, Syrah, Cabernet Sauvignon, Tempranillo, Pinot Gris and Zinfandel. The South Coast, with 3,000 acres of vineyards, starts in the Malibu-Newton Canyon AVA north of the city of Los Angeles and goes down to the southern border of California below San Diego. Among the 11 AVAs located in the region, the South Coast is the

Temecula Vineyard

largest. Other AVAs include Temecula Valley, Cucamonga Valley, Ramona Valley and San Pasqual Valley. Of the 100 wineries in the South Coast region, 40 of them are found in the Temecula Valley.

In addition to the regions mentioned above, I would ask you to consider trying some lesser known and equally delicious wines from Mendocino Ridge and Yorkville Highlands in Mendocino County; Calistoga, Coombsville, Oak Knoll District, Rutherford, Saint-Helena and Yountville in Napa; Petaluma Gap in Marin and Sonoma Counties; and Chalk Hill, Green Valley, Moon Mountain District and Sonoma Mountain from Sonoma County.

OTHER NOTABLE WINE REGIONS OF CALIFORNIA

Region/Area	Acres	Wineries	Grape Information	County
Livermore Valley	4,000	51	Cabernet Sauvignon, Chardonnay, Merlot, Petite Sirah	Alameda
Lake County	10,000	32	Cabernet Sauvignon, Sauvignon Blanc, Chardonnay, Merlot, Petite Sirah	Lake
Alexander Valley	15,000	39	Cabernet Sauvignon, Merlot, Chardonnay, Sauvignon Blanc, Zinfandel	Mendocino/Sonoma
Stag's Leap District	1,400	19	80% Cabernet Sauvignon and Merlot. Petite Sirah, Sangiovese, Sauvignon Blanc	Napa
St. Helena	9,200	156	Cabernet Sauvignon, Zinfandel, Cabernet Franc, Sauvignon Blanc, Sangiovese	Napa
Alexander Valley	15,000	39	Cabernet Sauvignon, Merlot, Chardonnay, Sauvignon Blanc, Zinfandel	Mendocino/Sonoma
Santa Cruz Mountains	1,500	75	Pinot Noir, Chardonnay, Cabernet Sauvignon, Merlot, Zinfandel	Santa Clara, Santa Cruz, San Mateo
Dry Creek Valley	9,000	70	27% Zinfandel, Cabernet Sauvignon, Chardonnay, Cabernet Franc, Petite Sirah	Sonoma
Green Valley	19,000	10	Chardonnay, Pinot Noir, Syrah, Zinfandel	Sonoma
Russian River Valley	15,000	110	41% Chardonnay, 29% Pinot Noir, Zinfandel, Merlot, Cabernet Sauvignon	Sonoma
Los Carneros	6,000	31	Chardonnay, Pinot Noir, Merlot, Syrah, Albarino/sparkling wine	Sonoma/Napa

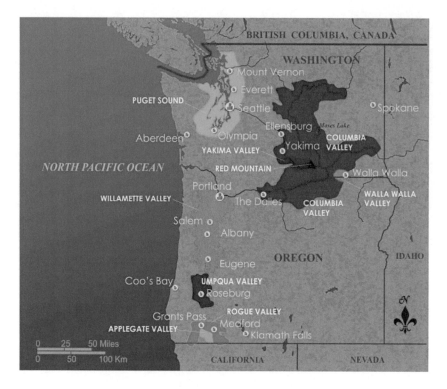

Map of Washington and Oregon

Washington

Grapes were first grown in Washington at Fort Vancouver in 1825. Today Washington is the second largest wine producer in the United States with over 825 wineries in 13 AVA regions and more than 50,000 acres of grape vines. Over 40 grape varieties are cultivated, with reds and whites grown in equal ratio. Merlot is the number one red grape variety grown here, with Syrah showing the most growth potential in the region and some Cabernet Sauvignon is cultivated as well. Other reds include Cabernet Franc, Malbec, Pinot Noir, and Sangiovese. Whites include Riesling, Chardonnay, Pinot Gris, Sauvignon Blanc, Gewürztraminer, Viognier, Sémillon and Chenin Blanc.

Most vineyards are planted inland in rather infertile valleys across the Cascades to the East. Eastern Washington has less than 10 inches of rainfall annually and an arid desert climate, with approximately 300 days of sunshine per year. The Columbia, Yakima and Snake rivers provide water for irrigation. The most damaging factor to note is the winter cold.

Washington has various soil types, including loess (a calcareous silt), volcanic basalt, clay, silt, loam and sandy loam.

COLUMBIA VALLEY

The Columbia Valley is Washington's largest wine region, covering one third of Washington's land mass. It contains 99 percent of the wine grapes grown in Washington, approximately 40,000 acres. In the Columbia Valley AVA, approximately 12,000 acres of vineyards are planted on predominantly south-facing slopes, which increases solar radiation in summer. There are today over 150 wineries. Riesling, Merlot, Chardonnay and Cabernet Sauvignon are the most widely planted varieties. The valley's vast size allows for a number of meso- and micro- climates. Most of the soil is basaltic sand, loess and river gravel.

YAKIMA VALLEY

Yakima Valley, which has more than 60 wineries, is Washington's first federally recognized appellation, and over one third of Washington's vineyards and 40 percent of its wine production take place here. There are 16,000 acres of planted vineyards. Chardonnay is the most widely planted grape, followed by Merlot and Cabernet Sauvignon. Riesling and Syrah represent a significant acreage and production of Syrah in particular is on the rise. Try a glass of red wine made of the rare Lemberger grape if you are in the area. Soil is silt-loam and sandy.

Sunset on Vineyard and Mount Adams

WALLA WALLA VALLEY

Grape growing in the Walla Walla Valley was established in the 1850s by Italian immigrants. Today it contains nearly 100 wineries and more than 1,600 acres of vineyards. The Walla Walla Valley is located in southeastern Washington and northeastern Oregon. Roughly 50 percent of the grapes grown in the Walla Walla Valley are grown in Oregon. Cabernet

Sauvignon is the leading variety here; Merlot, Chardonnay and Syrah are also predominant. Also grown in Walla Walla are Gewürztraminer, Cabernet Franc, Sangiovese, Grenache, Malbec, Petit Verdot, Tempranillo, Pinot Gris, Riesling, Sauvignon Blanc, Sémillon and Viognier. The soil here is loess.

Oregon

Oregon is the fourth largest wine producer in the United States, with 18 AVA regions and more than 600 wineries spanning over 25,000 acres and producing 72 varieties of grapes. The ratio of reds to whites is 65:35. Pinot Noir is the predominant grape variety grown throughout Oregon. Its northerly latitude means grapes get extra growing season sunlight, allowing for long, even ripening and crisp, cool nights.

In the marine-influenced Willamette Valley, Pinot Noir, Pinot Gris, Riesling and Chardonnay are the primary varieties grown. In the warm, high-elevation vineyards of Southern Oregon and the Walla Walla Valley, varieties include Cabernet Sauvignon, Tempranillo, Syrah and Viognier. In the Columbia Gorge and Eastern Oregon, varied microclimates allow winemakers and growers the luxury of working with the widest range of grape varieties of anywhere in the state. Below are Oregon's key wine regions.

WILLAMETTE VALLEY

The Willamette Valley is 150 miles long and up to 60 miles wide, making it Oregon's largest AVA and home to about 400 wineries. Close to 20,000 acres are planted with grape vines. It runs from the Columbia River in Portland south through Salem to the Calapooya Mountains outside Eugene, and is protected by the Coast Range to the west, the Cascades to the east and a series of hill chains to the north. Its namesake, the Willamette River, runs through its heart. The largest concentration of vineyards is located to the west of this river, on the slopes of the Coast Range. While most of the region's vineyards sit a few hundred feet above sea level, parts of the Willamette Valley do reach much higher. The Chehalem Mountains are the highest mountains in the valley, with their tallest point rising 1,633 ft (500 m) above sea level. The Willamette Valley has the largest concentration of wineries and vineyards in Oregon and includes six sub-appellations: Dundee Hills, Eola-Amity Hills, McMinnville, Ribbon Ridge,

Yamhill-Carlton and the recently approved Chehalem Mountains. Predominant varieties are Pinot Noir, Pinot Gris, Chardonnay and Riesling.

Modern winemaking in the Willamette Valley dates back 50 years and started with three UC Davis pioneers who believed that Oregon was an ideal place to grow cool-climate varieties and who were the first to plant Pinot Noir in the Willamette Valley. They also planted small amounts of Pinot Gris, Chardonnay and Riesling. The Willamette Valley became an official AVA in 1983. Today, it is recognized as one of the premier wine producing areas in the world. It is most widely known for its award winning Pinot Noir and consistently earns top honors for other such cool-climate varieties as Pinot Gris, Chardonnay and Pinot Blanc.

Vineyard in Morning Fog

The climate is relatively mild throughout the year, with cool, wet winters and warm, dry summers. Moisture is abundant, but most rainfall takes place during winter and not during the growing season. The gentle growing conditions within the valley are ideal for cool climate grapes like Pinot Noir. The Willamette Valley enjoys more daylight hours during the growing season than any other area of the state, and its warm days and cool nights allow the wine grapes to develop their flavor and complexity while retaining their natural acidity.

The Willamette Valley is an old volcanic and sedimentary seabed that has been overlaid with gravel, silt, rock and boulders. The most common of the volcanic type is red Jory soil, which is found at elevations above 300 ft. Anything below 300 ft is primarily sedimentary-based soil.

UMPQUA VALLEY

Umpqua Valley AVA sits between the Coast Range to the west and the Cascade Range to the east, with the Willamette Valley AVA to the north and the Rogue Valley AVA to the south. Named for the legendary fishing river that runs nearby, the appellation stretches 65 miles from north to south and is 25 miles from east to west. There are just under 1,000 acres of vineyards and 30 wineries. The Umpqua Valley's winegrowing history dates back to the late 1880s when German immigrants planted the first wine grape vineyard. The Umpqua Valley appellation became official in 1984. Predominant varieties are Pinot Noir, Pinot Gris, Riesling, Syrah, Tempranillo and Merlot.

The complex topography of the Umpqua Valley is a result of the collision of three mountain ranges of varying age and structure: the Klamath Mountains, the Coast Range and the Cascades. Many say the area should not be thought of as a single valley but, rather, more accurately "The Hundred Valleys of the Umpqua" because it is made up of a series of interconnecting small mountain ranges and valleys.

The Umpqua Valley can successfully grow both cool and warm climate grape varieties, as it is comprised of three distinct climatic sub-zones. The Northern area around the town of Elkton enjoys a cool, marine-influenced climate. It receives around 50 inches of annual rainfall, making irrigation unnecessary. The Central area to the northwest of Roseburg has a transitional, or intermediate, climate where both cool and warm varieties do quite well. The area south of Roseburg is warmer and more arid, similar to Rogue and Applegate valleys to the south, making irrigation necessary.

Umpqua Valley soils are a mix of sedimentary and volcanic rock. The valley floor levels have mostly deep alluvial or heavy clay materials, while the hillsides have mixed alluvial, silt or clay soil.

ROGUE VALLEY

The Rogue Valley AVA is the southernmost winegrowing region in Oregon. There are about 65 wineries with 2,400 acres of vineyards planted. It's made up of three adjacent river valleys (Bear Creek, Applegate and Illinois Valleys) that extend from the foothills of the Siskiyou Mountains along the California border north to the Rogue River. It is 70 miles wide by 60 miles long and encompasses the Applegate Valley sub-appellation. Rogue Valley's wine history dates back to the 1840s when European immigrants began planting grapes and eventually bottling wines. In the 1970s, winemakers rediscovered Rogue Valley as a superb winegrowing region. Rogue Valley became an official appellation in 2001.

The Rogue Valley, too, owes its diverse landscape to the convergence of the Klamath Mountains, the Coastal Range, and the Cascades; and includes the Rogue River. Vineyards here are typically at elevations of

1,200 to 2,000 ft (365 - 610 m) and are planted on hillsides rather than on the valley floor.

Rogue Valley is made up of three distinct valleys with progressively warmer microclimates, which enables the region to successfully grow both cool and warm-climate grape varieties. To the west, the region is affected by mountain and ocean influences, making it suitable for some cool-weather varieties, including Pinot Noir and Chardonnay. Farther east, Rogue Valley has the highest elevations of Oregon's winegrowing regions at nearly 2,000 ft (610 m), and it is also the warmest and the driest, making it well suited for warm-weather varieties including Merlot, Cabernet Sauvignon, Syrah and Sauvignon Blanc.

Rogue Valley soil types are many and varied, including mixes of metamorphic, sedimentary and volcanic derived soils ranging from sandy loam to hard clay.

New York

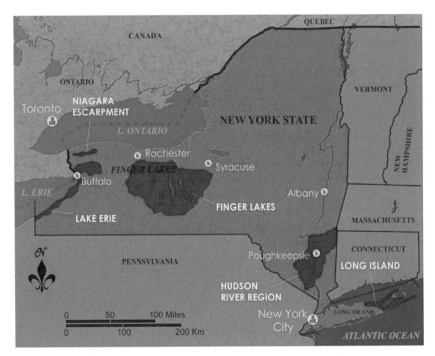

New York is the third largest wine producer in the United States. It has five primary AVAs that include the Finger Lakes, Niagara Escarpment, Hudson River, Long Island and Lake Erie. Each area has its own microclimate and *terroir* suitable for a total of 40 grape varieties grown here. There are over 1,600 family vineyards and around 375 wineries throughout the state, with half of them located in the Finger Lakes. *Vitis labrusca* accounts for approximately 75 percent of New York's grape area, which are primarily Concord grapes used for grape juice. *Vitis vinifera* makes up about 15 percent and French hybrids about 10 percent. Top red wine grape varieties grown in the state of New York are Merlot, Cabernet Franc, Cabernet Sauvignon, Pinot Noir, Baco Noir and Maréchal Foch. Top white varieties are Niagara, Catawba, Riesling, Chardonnay, Elvira, Seyval Blanc and Cayuga. Red wine makes up 50 percent of the State's production, followed by whites at 45 percent and rosés at five percent. There are a total of 37,000 acres of planted vineyards, with over 20,000 of them cultivating Concord grapes.

New York is known for its table wine, including the delicious Rieslings from the Finger Lakes, the well-balanced Merlots from Long Island and the sparkling wines and dessert wines which are the late harvest and Ice Wines.

FINGER LAKES

Riesling and Chardonnay dominate plantings in the Finger Lakes, with cooler temperatures and the massive lakes contributing to retaining the grapes' high acidity and clean aromatics. This region specializes in sparkling wine, table wine and Ice Wine. Table wine is made of Cabernet Franc, Merlot, Cabernet Sauvignon and Pinot Noir, as well as some French-American and Native American varietals. The soil is a shallow layer of topsoil on sloping shale beds.

HUDSON VALLEY

The Hudson River region is home to America's oldest continuously operating winery, Brotherhood Winery, which has been in operation since 1839. Most of the vineyards are within two miles of the Hudson River and are planted on steep hills. The most planted varieties are Chardonnay, Cabernet Franc, Seyval Blanc and other French-American varietals. The soil consists of glacial deposits of shale, slate, schist and limestone.

LONG ISLAND

The wines of Long Island use the same grapes as the Hudson River AVA, but often with a higher percentage of Cabernet Sauvignon. The climate is influenced by the Atlantic Ocean, resulting in earthy and lighter-bodied reds, while the whites tend to be acidic and herbaceous. Red grape varieties grown here include Merlot, Cabernet Sauvignon and Cabernet Franc. Whites include Chardonnay, Sauvignon Blanc, Gewürztraminer and some Riesling. The soil is sand.

NIAGARA ESCARPMENT

The geography of the Niagara Escarpment and surrounding area has a unique climate that is one of the warmest in New York State due to its proximity to two of the Great Lakes (Erie and Ontario) and the Escarpment itself, which traps warm air currents from Lake Ontario. The climate is very similar to the Niagara Peninsula in Ontario. The Niagara Escarpment was officially recognized as an AVA in 2005. Red grape varieties cultivated in this area are Pinot Noir, Syrah, and Cabernet Franc. Whites are Chardonnay, Riesling and white hybrids. The soil is limestone and gravel silt.

LAKE ERIE

The Lake Erie region is the third largest grape-growing region in the United States outside of California and Washington, with just under 20,000 acres of vineyards. The climate is affected by Lake Erie and the Allegheny Plateau. The predominant grape varieties are Seyval Blanc and Riesling. The soil is mainly gravely loam.

Vineyard at Sunset

CANADA

Canada extends 4,860 miles (7,820 km) from the Atlantic Ocean to the Pacific Ocean. It is known for its harsh winters, magnificent mountain ranges, large freshwater lakes, hockey and now its wines.

Canada is the world's 30th top wine producer and the number one producer of Icewine in the world. Seventy eight percent of Canadian wine comes from the Niagara Peninsula in Ontario; 18 percent comes from the Okanagan Valley in British Columbia some 2,560 miles (4,120 km) away. Five other Provinces produce wine but in far smaller quantities.

Ontario

Ontario is Canada's largest wine-producing province with over 180 wineries and 66 grape varieties. Ontario wineries produce world-class Icewine and excellent still and sparkling wines. Today, about 17,000 acres of vines produce approximately 70 percent of Canadian wine.

Ontario wine labels use the term "Vintners Quality Alliance (VQA)". The VQA (established in 1988) is a regulatory and appellation system used to guarantee that a wine from Ontario is both authentic and of high quality. The VQA designation also indicates that the wine was made in Ontario. All VQA wines are verified to confirm their origin and tested to ensure they meet a rigorous set of quality standards. Wines made from 100 percent Ontario grapes can qualify for classification under the VQA.

For Purposes of Illustration Only

Three official wine-growing regions, known as Designated Viticultural Areas (DVAs), are recognized and regulated by the VQA. They are the Niagara Penisula, Lake Erie North Shore and Prince Edward County. Notice that the above sample label indicates that the wine is from the Niagara Peninsula DVA.

Southern Ontario grape growers face a number of challenges, including harsh winters and fungal diseases created by its humid summers. One of my favorite Ontario sights in winter is the use of wind machines in vineyards to help reduce both the cold and frost injury to vines.

The predominant grapes for red wine and rosé production are Cabernet Franc, Merlot, Pinot Noir, Gamay, Cabernet Sauvignon and Baco Noir. The most planted white grapes are Riesling, Chardonnay, Pinot Gris, Sauvignon Blanc and Gewürztraminer. For Icewines and late harvest wines the main grape varieties are Vidal, Riesling, Cabernet Franc and to a lesser degree Cabernet Sauvignon. Approximately 60 percent of grapes grown in Ontario are white and 40 percent are red. Over 65 percent of Ontario wine is produced from *Vitis vinifera* grapes.

Climatic conditions across wine regions in Ontario vary widely, and it is worth noting that there are distinct differences between appellations (DVAs) and the Niagara sub-appellations.

NIAGARA PENINSULA

The Niagara Peninsula is Canada's largest wine-growing region, located in southern Ontario about an hour from Toronto, Ontario and Buffalo, NY. It boasts 14,850 acres and has a unique micro-climate that is influenced by both the Niagara Escarpment and impressive Lake Ontario. These geographical features result in moderate spring and summer temperatures which, coupled with its rich and fertile silt and clay loam soils, make Niagara a prime region for the cultivation of grapes.

Winter Vineyard at Sunset

Niagara is divided into two regional appellations and ten sub-appellations, with each having unique growing conditions suited to different grape varieties.

There are 83 wineries and 32 grape varieties cultivated in this region, the most prominent grapes being Riesling, Chardonnay, Merlot, Cabernet Franc, Cabernet Sauvignon and Pinot Noir. Icewine is made of Riesling and Vidal. Red Icewine is produced from Cabernet Franc.

British Columbia

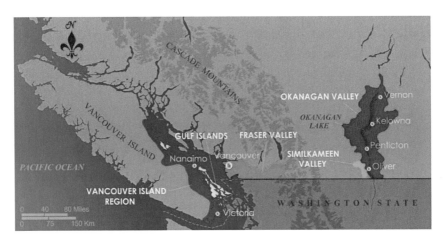

British Columbia is Canada's second largest wine-growing province with 254 wineries and over 80 grape varieties. Based on their unique *terroir*, there are six official viticultural areas in the province, called Geographical Indications (GIs) and recognized by the British Columbia Vintners Quality Alliance (BC VQA). They are the province of British Columbia as a whole, the Okanagan Valley, the Similkameen Valley, Vancouver Island, Fraser Valley and the Gulf Islands.

BC VQA certified wines meet rigorous standards with respect to origin, vintage and varietals, and prior to displaying the BC VQA designation on their labels, they must also pass a taste test to verify quality characteristics. The grapes used must be 100 percent grown in British Columbia. If a specific region is mentioned on the label, then 95 percent of the grapes in the wine must have originated from that region. If the label includes a vintage then 85 percent of the grapes must come from that vintage. Additionally, 85 percent of the grapes used must be the stated variety. Wines produced from British Columbia grapes that have not gone through the BC VQA Certification Process are considered "Wines of Distinction" and may be labeled "Product of British Columbia".

Most British Columbia vineyards are located to the east of the Cascade Mountains. The weather in these south-eastern regions is mild and relatively wet, while further to the east, in the Similkameen and the Okanagan wine regions, the "rain shadow" affect creates substantially warmer and drier conditions. To the west of the Cascade Mountain Range and closer to the Pacific Ocean, wineries are scattered throughout the Vancouver Island Region, the Gulf Islands and the Fraser Valley Region.

The most prominent red grape varieties are Merlot, Pinot Noir, Cabernet Sauvignon, Cabernet Franc and Syrah; followed by Gamay Noir, Maréchal Foch, Malbec, Petit Verdot and Zweigelt. The most prominent white wine grape varieties are Pinot Gris, Chardonnay, Gewürztraminer, Riesling and Sauvignon Blanc, followed by Pinot Blanc, Viognier, Muscats, Ehrenfelser and Ortega. British Columbia wineries produce excellent Icewine as well as delicious table, late-harvest, fortified and sparkling wines.

OKANAGAN VALLEY

The Okanagan Valley is the most notable northern wine region in the world, stretching 150 miles (250 km) along a chain of fresh water lakes from Armstrong, British Columbia south to the Washington State border. It is a hot, dry desert with limestone soil. The majority of grapes grown here include Sauvignon Blanc, Pinot Gris, Riesling and Gewürztraminer. Over 84 percent of the total vineyard acreage in the province of British Columbia is grown here. The interior of British Columbia has a mild and dry climate which is ideal for growing grapes, and the Okanagan Valley in particular is known for its high quality wines.

Okanagan Vineyards

There are 744 vineyards and 163 wineries here, with over 8,600 acres of planted grape vines.

Québec

Southern Québec is comprised of six distinct regions: the Eastern Townships, Montérégie, Québec, Basses Laurentides, Lanaudière and Centre-du-Québec. Presently there are over 110 wineries growing more than 15 grape varieties. Although grapes have been cultivated in Québec for the last two centuries, it is only since the 1980s that local wine production has seen a steady increase. The wines produced by Québec's cottage wineries are equally divided between whites and reds. Most wine is consumed within the province itself.

Much of what is produced in Québec is based on hybrid grape varieties such as Vidal, Sainte-Croix, Maréchal Foch and the white and red grapes of both Seyval and Frontenac. Less well known varieties for red wine are: Marquette, Léon Millot, Sabrevois, De Chaunac, Lucy Kulman and Baco Noir; and for white wine: Frontenac Gris, Vandal-Cliche, Cayuga and St-Pépin. Both Chardonnay and Riesling are also planted.

Because of their cold climate and very long winters, growers in Québec began planting below-zero-temperature-resistant grape varieties in the 1980s. Additionally, in early November, to protect them from the cold, a plow is used to pile soil 1.6 ft (50 cm) high at the base of the vines. This soil is removed in the spring to allow the base to breathe properly. The soil in Québec is sand and gravel.

In 1987, the first few Québec wine growers formed an association called *l'Association des Vignerons du Québec.* Since 2009, this has been a voluntary certification. The primary goal of the certification program is full traceability from the bottle to the grape harvest. The certification used in Québec is actually similar to the VQA in Ontario except that in order to receive certification, an independent, third-party auditor must pass through the vineyard every year to validate the process. Additionally, in order to place on the wine label *"Vins Certifiés du Québec"*, the wine must be certified and pass with success through the *"comité d'agrément"* or blind tasting. All grapes must be 100 percent from the province of Québec.

Québec wine is produced in a number of styles, including dry, semi-dry and vin doux natural. Additionally, the region offers Ice Wine (*vin de glace*), late harvest wine and sparkling wine.

Nova Scotia

Nova Scotia is a peninsula on the east coast of Canada that lies between the Bay of Fundy and the North Atlantic Ocean, and grapes have been grown here for wine since the 1600s. It is best known for its crisp, refreshing, aromatic whites and its world class sparkling wines. The six distinct wine-growing regions in Nova Scotia are Annapolis Valley, Avon River Valley, Bear River Valley, Gaspereau Valley, LaHave River Valley and the Northumberland Coast.

The soil and weather in Nova Scotia are ideal for growing grapes, and Nova Scotia is home to 17 wineries and over 30 varieties. Hybrids are still the most predominantly grown, including the white hybrid grape L'Acadie Blanc, which does very well here, the New York Muscat and the Maréchal Foch. L'Acadie Blanc is "the quintessential Nova Scotia grape," says Gaspereau's winemaker, Gina Haverstock. For red wine, Léon Millot, Castel, Marquette and Luci Kuhlman are the most widely used hybrid varieties. Many wineries and vintners are also having increasing success with *Vitis vinifera* grapes such as Chardonnay, Riesling, Pinot Gris, Ortega, Baco Noir and Pinot Noir. Sixty percent of the grapes grown here are white, the remaining are red.

The Winery Association of Nova Scotia (WANS) was established in 2002, and there is one appellation in Nova Scotia called Tidal Bay. Wines made with 100 percent Nova Scotia grapes can place the words "Nova Scotia" on their label.

The soil in Nova Scotia is siltstone, shale, sandstone, basalt and limestone and the climate is cool Maritime.

Other Provinces

Other areas where wines are produced include New Brunswick, Prince Edward Island and Newfoundland.

FRANCE

The more specific the name, the better the wine.
Frank Schoonmaker

France is the standard for fine wine by which other wine producing nations are measured today and have been measured for decades. France is the number one wine producer in the world and is among the countries that drink the most wine per capita. France's geography and climate are perfect for viniculture. French wines are distinguished by regions and districts, not by grape varieties. Approximately 56 grape varieties are grown in France.

Before we tour the wonderful regions of France it is important to define three key words: *Grand Cru, Domaine* and *Négociant. Grand Cru* is the highest classification of French wine. *Domaine* is basically the French term for wine estate. Labels that state *mis en bouteille au domaine* distinguish wine that has been bottled at the wine estate from wine bottled at cooperatives. Co-ops produce wine by mixing together grapes brought from multiple estates. *Négociant* is the French term for "merchant" or "dealer". It is used in the wine world to refer to a person or a firm that sells and ships wine as a wholesaler. Some labels contain *négociant-éleveur,* to distinguish a wine where the merchant-grower blends several varieties together. *Eleveur* means grower or, in this case, producer.

Quality Levels and Appellation System

In 1935, France passed laws to control the quality of French wine and the French *Appellation d'Origine Contrôlée* (AOC) system was established. In 2012 the qualification system was updated. It is still important to know the earlier appellation system should you come in contact with a bottle labeled prior to 2012. Up until 2012, the official tiers of French wine quality classification were the following.

AOC indicated the geographical origin, quality and (generally) the style of a wine. All Grand Cru and Premier Cru wines fell into the AOC category. Grand Cru can refer to a wine in one of two ways. It is either the plot of land where the grapes are grown, which applies in Burgundy, Alsace, Champagne, Languedoc-Rousillon and the Loire Valley, or it is the château where the wine is made, although this designation is exclusive to the Bordeaux Region. Premier Cru denotes either a vineyard plot (most common in Burgundy) of superior quality, or the very highest tier within a Grand Cru classification (such as the *Premier Grand Cru Classé* châteaux of Bordeaux).

The VDQS (*Vin Délimité de Qualité Supérieure*) designation was not as strict as AOC. It was used for smaller areas, or as the next step to obtaining the AOC status. This category was dropped in 2011.

Vin de Pays means "wine of the country." This category focuses on geographical origin rather than style and tradition and notes the specific region within France (for example *Vin de Pays d'Oc* from Languedoc-Roussillon) from which the wine originated. Regulations were less restrictive than for AOC wines.

Vin de Table, meaning "table wine" was the most basic quality tier for French wine.

Most Recent Major Changes

In the new French wine classification system there are three categories rather than four, as the category corresponding to VDQS was dropped. The new categories are *Appellation d'Origine Protégée* (AOP), the highest category replacing AOC wines; *Indication Géographique Protégée* (IGP), an intermediate category replacing the term *Vin de Pays;* and *Vin de France*, which replaces *Vin de Table*. It is permitted to indicate the grape variety and vintage on the label.

Although this new system is simpler, the change in name and category level has caused some confusion among wine producers and purchasers alike. Whereas *Vin de Pays*, which means "wine of the country," was the intermediate category, *Vin de France*, meaning "wine of France" (France being the country), is now the lowest category.

Burgundy (Bourgogne)

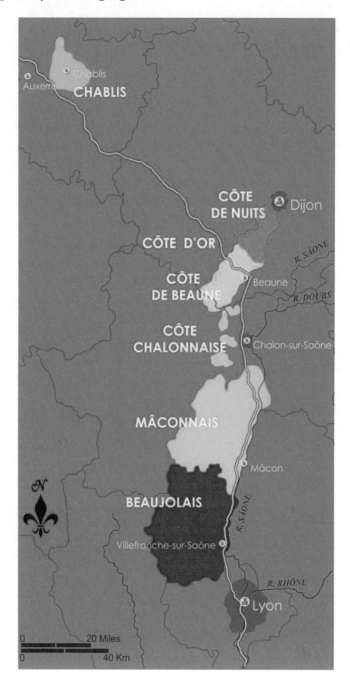

Burgundy is without a doubt one of the most famous wine regions in the world. It is comprised of five smaller districts.

CHABLIS

Chablis is halfway between la Côte d'Or and Paris, where white wines, mostly Chardonnay, are produced with a crisper and steelier style than IN the rest of Burgundy. It should be noted that Chablis also has its own wine classification system, set apart from the rest of Burgundy. In short, there is Petit Chablis, Chablis, Premier Cru Chablis and Grand Cru Chablis. The Grand Crus of the Chablis Region include les Bougerots, les Preuses, Vaudésir, les Grenouilles, Valmur, les Clos and Blanchot.

CÔTE D'OR

Côte d'Or, which means "golden slope" or "hill", is comprised of two areas that include Côte de Nuits in the north and Côte de Beaune in the south, with Chardonnay and Pinot Noir the main grape varieties. You will also find Aligoté, Pinot Gris, Pinot Blanc, Sauvignon Blanc and Melon de Bourgogne.

French Village in Burgundy Vineyards

CÔTE DE NUITS

Côte de Nuits is home to 24 Grand Cru vineyards and some of the world's most expensive vineyard real estate. Most of the vineyards are relatively small in surface. The area begins south of Dijon and ends at the village of Corgoloin. Eighty percent of the wines produced here are Pinot Noir and the remaining 20 percent are Chardonnay and Marsannay. Appellations include Marsannay (delicious rosés), Fixin, Gevrey-Chambertin, Morey-St-Denis, Chambolle-Mussigny, Vougeot, Vosne-Romanée and Nuit-Saint-Georges.

CÔTE DE BEAUNE

Côte de Beaune is named after the quaint medieval village that is the heart of wine commerce in Burgundy. When I lived in Geneva, Switzerland, every two weeks or so I would spend a weekend in the Burgundy region to visit vineyards and eat at some of the best restaurants in France. I made sure to visit the town of Beaune, which is absolutely enchanting. In Côte de Beaune, the vineyards have more of a southeasterly exposure and Chardonnay plays a more important role, with seven of the eight Grand Cru vineyards

The Beaune Hospice

producing white wine. Vineyards include Ladoix, Pernand-Vergelesses, Aloxe-Corton, Chorey-les-Beaune, Savigny-les-Beaune, Monthelie, Meursault, Auxey-Duresses, Saint-Romain, Puligny-Montrachet, Beaune (a quaint and historic town where the food is delicious), Pommard, Volnay, Saint-Aubin (I love the wines from this area, as they have a great quality to price ratio), Chassagne-Montrachet, Santenay and Maranges. Chardonnays from the town of Puligny-Montrachet are among my very favorite on earth.

CÔTE CHALONNAISE

Côte Chalonnaise is located between the towns of Chagny and Saint-Vallerin. Chardonnay is the leading grape. This area does not have any Grand Cru vineyards. The first village in the northern part of the region is Bouzeron, and it is the only appellation devoted to the other white grape of Burgundy known as Aligoté. The vineyards include Bouzeron, Rully, Mercurey, Givry and Montagny.

MÂCONNAIS

Mâconnais is the largest region of Burgundy proper. Chardonnay is again the leading grape. Located between the town of Tournus and Saint-Véran, it lies at the crossroads of Northern and Southern France. The climate is warmer, so the harvest begins two weeks earlier than in Chablis. Well known areas include Pouilly-Fuissé, Pouilly-Vinzelles, Pouilly-Loché and Saint-Véran.

Beaujolais

Beaujolais is in the southern-most part of Burgundy proper, located north of Lyon and covering parts of the north of the Rhône. I have visited this area many times, as the small towns and vineyards are very special, the people kind and the food exquisite. Its climate is closer to that of the Rhône region. The red wine is generally made of the Gamay grape, while whites from the region make up only one percent of its total production and are made mostly with Chardonnay grapes and, to a small degree, Aligoté. During some vintages, Beaujolais produces more wine than the other Burgundy wine regions of Chablis, Côte d'Or, Côte Chalonnaise and Mâconnais *combined*. Ten Beaujolais Crus produce delicious light red wines. Juliénas, Saint-Amour, Chénas, Moulin-à-Vent, Brouilly, Fleurie, Chiroubles, Morgon, Régnié and Côte-de-Brouilly. This region is also known for its Beaujolais Nouveau.

The climate in Burgundy is Continental to mild Continental with some Mediterranean influence. The soil is limestone, marl (limy clay), sand, granite and Kimmeridgian clay. Red grape varieties grown are predominantly Pinot Noir and Gamay. White grape varieties are primarily Chardonnay, Aligoté and Muscadet.

Label Classification

The variation in soil and climate (*terroir*) between Burgundy's many vineyard sites is the basis of the region's wine classification system. The more specific the region or area, the better the wine; the higher the percentage of production, the lower the quality. See examples below.

Growth	English	Name	Percent of Production	Number of Vineyards
Grand Cru	Great Growth	Le Montrachet	2	33
Premier Cru	First Growth	Pulligny-Montrachet Les Pucelles	12	562
Communale AOPs	Village	Pulligny-Montrachet	36	41
Régionale AOPs	Regional	Bourgogne Blanc	50	23

Bordeaux

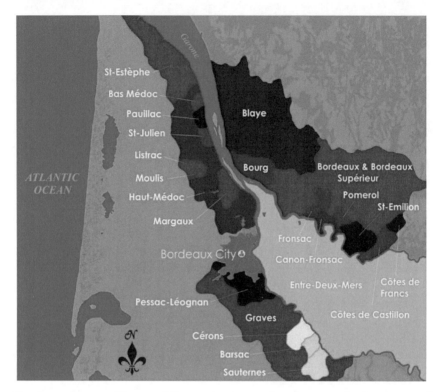

Bordeaux is one of the world's most renowned regions, producing many of the world's greatest wines, with a production quantity of 500 to 700 million bottles annually. Seventy-five percent of production is red wines. Bordeaux is over twice as large as the Burgundy wine region.

Vineyards in Bordeaux are known as châteaux, which means castles. These are single ownership estates. There are over 3,000 châteaux names in Bordeaux.

Bordeaux is separated by two rivers: the Gironde and the Dordogne. Areas on the Left Bank (primarily Cabernet Sauvignon blends) include Médoc, Saint-Estèphe, Pauillac, Saint-Julien, Haut-Médoc, Margaux, Péssac-Léognan, Graves, Barsac and Sauternes. My personal "desert island" wine is a red Saint-Estèphe. See the French label on page 60.

Areas on the Right Bank (primarily Merlot blends) include Saint-Emilion, Pomerol, Fronsac, Canon-Fronsac, Côtes de Bourg, Côtes de Blaye, Entre-Deux-Mers and Saint-Croix-du-Mont.

As Cabernet Franc is principally grown for blending with Cabernet Sauvignon and Merlot in the Bordeaux style, it is worth noting, *mes amis*, that the following super high end wines from the Saint-Emilion and Pomerol regions each contain over 45 percent Cabernet Franc: Château Cheval Blanc, Château Ausone and Château Angélus. These three wines command some of the world's highest prices.

The climate of Bordeaux is maritime with a strong Atlantic influence. Soil is gravel with limestone subsoil, sand and flat pebbles with clay and limestone. Red grape varieties are Cabernet Sauvignon, Merlot, Cabernet Franc, Malbec (Côtes de Bourg), *Carménère* and Petit Verdot. White varieties are Sémillon and Sauvignon Blanc.

Roses are the "canary in the coal mine" for mildew in the vineyards.

Label Terms

In 1855, a panel of Bordeaux wine brokers agreed to compile a list of the best wines in the region for Napoleon III's Universal Exposition in Paris. Two weeks after receiving their task, the brokers returned a list with 58 wines—57 of them from the Médoc region in Bordeaux. While the red wines were given five distinct classes from First Growth (*Premier Cru*) to Fifth Growth (*Cinquième Cru*), the white Sauternes and Barsac only received First and Second Growth distinctions, with one exception: Château d'Yquem from Sauternes was the only wine to receive the Great First Growth distinction, or *Grand Premier Cru*. The First Growth (Premier Cru) wines of the Médoc Region on the Left Bank are:

Name	District	Year
Lafite-Rothschild	Pauillac	1855
Margaux	Margaux	1855
Latour	Pauillac	1855
Haut-Brion	Graves and Pessac-Leognan	1855
Mouton-Rothschild	Pauillac	Promoted from second to first growth in 1973

The First Great Growths (*Premiers Grands Crus Classés*) of the 1955 Classification of Saint-Emilion on the Right Bank are Ausone and Cheval Blanc. In the 2012 classification, two more Châteaux became members: Château Angélus and Château Pavie.

Chateau in the Vineyards

The Pomerol Region has no official classification, but has two notable wines: Château Pétrus and Château Le Pin. They are often considered to be at the same level of quality as the first growths of the 1855 classification and are two of the most expensive wines on earth.

Languedoc-Roussillon

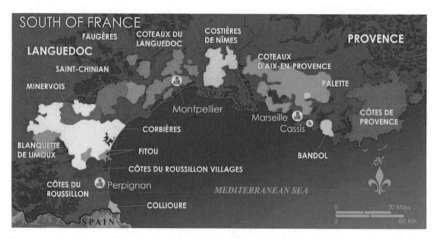

Languedoc-Roussillon is one of the most interesting regions in southwestern France in that it offers all types of wines and, with improved technology, better quality year to year. Languedoc-Roussillon is the largest region in terms of both vineyard surface area and production. The area is known for its delicious sweet wines with the appellation *Vins Doux Naturels (VDN)*. The whites are made from Muscat à Petits Grains or Muscat d'Alexandre (my younger son's name) and the reds from Grenache. The climate in Languedoc-Roussillon is Mediterranean with cool mistral winds. The soil is marly limestone, shale, clay and gravel.

Regions with AOP include Côteaux du Languedoc, Faugères, Saint-Chinian, Minervois, Corbières, Fitou, Côtes du Roussillon and Collioure. Regions with VDN are Muscat de Mireval, de Frontignan, de Saint-Jean-de-Minervois, de Rivesaltes, Limoux, Maury and Banyuls.

Red grapes grown here include Carignan, Grenache, Cinsault and Syrah, with Cabernet Sauvignon and Merlot as newcomers to this region. White grape varieties are Grenache Blanc, Mauzac, Clairette, Muscat and Bourboulenc.

LABEL TERMS

Label terms coming out of Languedoc-Roussillon include AOP and VDN. VDN wines are lightly fortified wines typically made from white Muscat grapes or red Grenache grapes in the south of France, e.g., Languedoc-Roussillon.

Chapel in a Vineyard

The Loire Valley

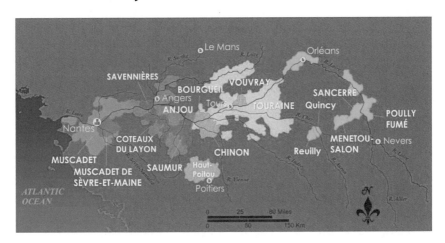

The Loire Valley is one of the most beautiful wine regions in the world. It is home to a great deal of history, stunning châteaux and charming villages. Food here is spectacular. I spent one week in the area and it was not nearly enough. Without a doubt it would have required at least two weeks to put a tiny dent

Saumur Castle and Vineyards

into seeing all this region has to offer. It is the largest white wine region in France and the second largest for sparkling wine. The Loire Valley is the only region in France to produce excellent wines of every variety: red, white, rosé, still, sparkling, dry and sweet. The Loire Valley includes wine regions located along the Loire River from the Muscadet region near the city of Nantes on the Atlantic coast to the region of Sancerre in north central France. In between are the regions of Anjou, Saumur, Bourgueil, Chinon and Vouvray. The climate in the Loire Valley is Maritime to Continental. The soil is *Tuffeau blanc* (chalky freestone), slate, shale, gravel, limestone, sandy, alluvial flood-plain, clay, Kimmerridgian formations and flint.

Muscadet, also known as *Melon de Bourgogne,* is grown in the region of Nantais; Chenin Blanc, Cabernet Franc and Gamay in the region of Anjou-Saumur; Sauvignon Blanc, Gamay, Cabernet Franc and Chenin Blanc in Touraine; and Sauvignon Blanc and Pinot Noir in the Central Vineyards. Other varieties grown include Cabernet Sauvignon, Malbec and Groslot (reds); Grolleau and Pinot Gris (rosés); and Chardonnay and Chasselas (whites).

Label terms are IGP and *Jardin de la France.*

Alsace

In October of 1983, I left Geneva to spend four days in the Alsace region. My goal? Same as always—food and wine—and I was not disappointed. I ate at two of the nicest restaurants I had ever been to; one was in Illhaeusern and the other in Strasbourg. The landscape was picturesque, the charming towns were straight from a movie, and the wine was refreshing with a minerality that was an absolute joy to drink.

Alsace has very little rainfall because it is sheltered from prevailing rain-bearing winds by the Vosges Mountains. It also experiences a considerable amount of sun (120 days per year), which is most unusual for this part of Europe. You may one day wish to visit this region, as it offers such interesting history and the towns could not be more picturesque. Due to its strong German influence, it is the only region in France to produce mostly varietally labeled wines: Riesling, Pinot Gris and Gewürztraminer. Approximately 90 percent of the wines grown in Alsace are white. You will also find soft rosés made of Pinot Noir, which is the only red grape variety authorized in the region. The climate is Continental, and the soil is limestone, marly clay, sandstone, granite and volcanic soil.

There are 25 wine-growing districts in Alsace: Altenberg de Bergheim, Kanzlerberg, Osterberg, Kirchberg de Ribeauville, Geisberg, Rosacker, Froehn, Schonenbourg, Sporen, Sonnenglanz, Mandelberg, Marckrain, Mambourg, Furstentum, Schlossberg, Wineck- Schlossberg, Sommerberg, Florimont, Brand, Hengst, Steingrubler, Pfersigberg, Eichberg, Hatschbourg and Goldert.

Alsace Village in Vineyard

Just about all wine production is Alsace AOP, since there is no IGP in this region. Label terms include: *Crémant d'Alsace AOP; Alsace Grand Cru AOP; Vendange Tardive* (VT), which is the French term for "late harvest"; and *Sélection de Grains Nobles* (SGN). *Sélection de Grains Nobles* wines are sweet dessert wines. It is French for "selection of noble berries" and refers to wines made from grapes affected by Noble Rot.

The Rhône Valley

The Rhône Valley, in the southeast of France, is found along the Rhône River. The Northern Region has a reputation for the highest quality wines, and only five percent of the entire Rhône Valley production is made here. Topsoil is washed down the hills or slopes (*les côtes*) by heavy rain and carried back up to the top to fill the terraces by hand or machinery, depending on the degree of the slope.

Northern wine areas are Côte-Rotie (which means "toasted hill" because the sun hits with such intensity), Condrieu, Hermitage (the oldest vineyard in France), Crozes-Hermitage (which produces the most sought after Rhône reds), Saint-Joseph, Cornas (underappreciated, it is one of the smallest appellations in the Rhône valley and produces only red wine) and Saint-Peray. Syrah is the red grape cultivated here. The whites are Viognier, Marsanne and Roussanne and the latter two are a real pleasure to drink if you can find them. The climate is Continental with Mediterranean influence and strong mistral winds that have serious effects on vineyards. The soil is crystalline, rocky, mica-schist and granite.

The Southern Region produces an impressive 95 percent of the entire Rhône production, and it is also home to the wonderful Châteauneuf-du-Pape wines, which may contain up to 13 grape varieties and is one of my favorite red wines. Muscat de Beaumes-de-Venise is a delicious, sweet, fortified wine made of the white Muscat grapes of the type VDN.

Côtes-du-Rhône Vineyards

Southern wine areas are Côtes du Vivarais, Côtes du Rhône-Villages, Lirac, Tavel (which produces gorgeous rosé wines), Châteauneuf-du-Pape (shortened to CdP), Vacqueyras (an up-and-coming region and appellation—excellent quality for the price), Gigondas, Côteaux du Tricastin, Côtes du Ventoux and Côtes du Luberon. Grenache is the predominant red grape grown here, followed by Syrah and Cinsault. Carignan and Mourvèdre are minor varieties. White grapes are Clairette, Muscat and Grenache Blanc.

The climate in the Southern Region is Mediterranean with hot summers and drought can be a problem in the area. The soil is heavy clay, limestone and stony alluvial deposits.

AOP on the label of wines produced in The Rhône Valley indicates the geographical origin, quality and (generally) the style of a wine.

Provence

Located in southeast France along the coast of the Mediterranean, Provence is bordered by the Rhône River to the west and by La Côte d'Azur on the east. It is close to Cannes (think film festival) and Marseilles and is another great destination given its rugged terrain, delicious Mediterranean food and refreshing rosés. It is the oldest wine-producing region in France. Provence is a very warm, sunny and hilly region that receives approximately 280 days of sun a year. Eighty percent of the wine produced in this region is rosé. The climate in Provence is Mediterranean with mistral winds. Soil is stony limestone, sandstone, clay, shale and gravel.

The regions of Provence are Côtes de Provence, Côteaux d'Aix-en-Provence, Palette, Bandol (best known for its serious and age-worthy wines made mostly from the Mourvèdre grape), Cassis, Bellet, Côteaux Varois and Les Baux-de-Provence. Red grape varieties are Grenache, Carignan, Cinsault, Mourvèdre, Syrah and Cabernet Sauvignon. Rosé grape varieties are Grenache, Cinsault and Mourvèdre. White grape varieties are Ugni Blanc, Clairette, Sémillon, Grenache Blanc, Sauvignon Blanc and Tibouren. Label term is *AOP*.

Champagne

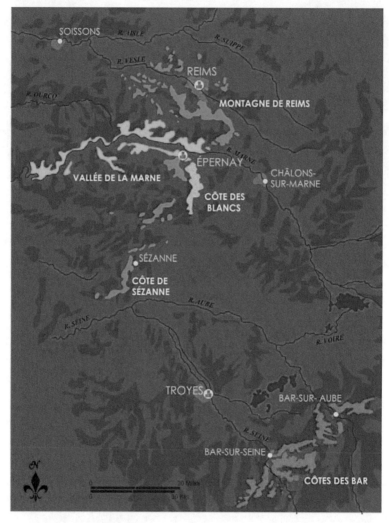

Champagne is located 100 miles (160 km) northeast of Paris. Fourth Century Romans dug the Caves where many of today's makers store their wine. These chalk caves keep the wine at a constant 53°F/12°C and 88 percent humidity. The cool climate outside the caves does not allow Chardonnay, Pinot Meunier and Pinot Noir to fully ripen. This results in grapes with higher acidity and lighter flavors that are perfect for Champagne. Champagne wines can be white, rosé and sometimes red.

Méthode champenoise/méthode traditionnelle wines are made in two fermentations. A still wine is created and then bottled with added yeast and sugar before it is closed off with a beer cap. The additives affect a second fermentation, a by-product of which is carbon dioxide. Since the bottle is closed off, the carbon dioxide cannot escape and it dissolves into the wine, creating the bubbles that are known as pearls. The wine is aged for a minimum of eighteen months. Then the bottles are riddled either manually or mechanically.

During the riddling process, the yeast and other sediment in the bottle are slowly worked into the neck where they can be removed during the disgorging (*dégorgement*) process. Madame Clicquot (Veuve Clicquot means "widow Clicquot") invented this process in 1816, during which the extra sediment and yeast are frozen in the neck of the bottle, expelled and quickly replaced with extra wine and sugar.

Champagne Cellar

The climate in Champagne is cold and wet Continental. The soil is mostly chalk, limestone, clay and sand. Regions are Montagne de Reims, Vallée de la Marne, Côte des Blancs, Aube, Côte des Bars and Côte de Sézanne. Pinot Noir and Pinot Meunier are the red grapes grown here and about two thirds of Champagne is made of these two varieties. The other third of Champagne is made from Chardonnay grapes. Label terms are Grand Cru (17 villages) and Premier Cru (41 villages).

ITALY

Italy is ranked second in terms of wine production, with more grape varieties than any other country in the world. In fact, there are approximately 800 grape varieties in Italy, of which 350 to 360 have been granted "authorized" status. Nonetheless, as stated in the excellent book *Vino Italiano, The Regional Wines of Italy,* by Joseph Bastianich and David Lynch, "the 500 or so that are not authorized (by Italy's Ministry of Agriculture and Forestry (MIRAF)), are finding their way into some of the wines we drink and may factor even more prominently in the future." There are primarily 67 grape varieties grown in Italy today. Chianti is the oldest protected wine region in the world (since 1716).

Italy is one of my favorite countries to visit. Each region offers the traveler something different: architecture, history, landscape, food and *naturalmente* wine. I had the pleasure of visiting Piedmont, Tuscany, Umbria and Veneto a few times and I would return tomorrow morning for a week or two at a moment's notice.

Of the red grapes grown here, Sangiovese, Italy's claim to fame, is from Tuscany, which also produces Chianti. Nebbiolo is the most noble of Italy's grape varieties and Merlot, Barbera, Montepulciano and Primitivo (Zinfandel) are also grown here. Aglianico is considered the noble grape of the south of Italy. Dolcetto, Nero d'Avola, Negroamaro, Malvasia Nera, Nerello, Lambrusco, Corvina, Rondinella, Molinara, Schiava, Lagrein, Refosco, Teroldego are other lesser-known varieties. I suggest you taste four of my very favorite Italian red wines: Barolo, Barbaresco, Brunello di Montalcino and Amarone.

Of the white grape varieties planted in Italy, Cataratto Bianco and Trebbiano are the two most predominant. Verdicchio is named from the word "verde" which means green. Pinot Grigio, Cortese, Grechetto, Verdello, Malvasia, Vernaccia, Garganega, Inzolia, Moscato, Nuragus and Tocai Friulino are also cultivated .

The Italian climate varies from Continental to Continental Alpine, Mild, Temperate, Arid and Mediterranean. Soil is clay, sand, gravel, limestone, sandstone, alluvial deposits, schist, granite, volcanic rock, sandy, shale, chalky and calcareous clay.

Italy has 20 wine regions which correspond to its 20 administrative regions, Piedmont, Tuscany and Veneto being the top-producing regions. Italian wines rank among the world's best.

Piedmont (Piemonte)

Piedmont is the mountainous range that produces the wines made in the northwestern corner of Italy. Red grape varieties grown here are Barbera, Brachetto, Dolcetto and Nebbiolo. Whites are Arneis, Cortese, Erbaluce, Moscato, Chardonnay and Muscat à Petits Grains.

Autumnal Vineyards in Piedmont

Piedmont is known for its wonderful wines made of Nebbiolo grapes. Barolo is known as "the king" of Piedmont wines and Barbaresco "the queen". Gattinara and Ghemme wines are also made of Nebbiolo grapes. There are 48 grape varieties grown in this region. The climate is Continental with cold winds; the soil is sandstone and clay.

Veneto

Veneto grows 51 grape varieties, the most in all of Italy, and it is well-known for its still, white Soave, made from Garganega and Trebbiano di Soave grapes grown in the hills between Lake Garda and the town of Soave. Recioto della Valpolicella DOCG (see page 121) is also recognized as one of Italy's finest sweet wines.

Corvina is the finest of the three major red grapes from this region, followed by Molinara and Rondinella. Cabernet Sauvignon, Cabernet Franc, Carménère, Raboso and Merlot are also grown here. White grape varieties include Garganega, Trebbiano, Glera (Prosecco), Dolcetto, Trebbiano di Soave, Chardonnay, Tocai Friulano, Riesling and Pinot Blanc.

Valpolicella is the easy-drinking red blend of Corvina, Rondinella and Molinara grapes. Bardolino, a different blend from the same three grapes, is known for its smooth character. A third blend of these grapes, the deep, dark Amarone della Valpolicella, known simply as Amarone and recently promoted to DOCG (see page 121) status, is one of my favorite red wines. The grapes are partly dried, in a traditional manner, on straw mats. Amarone is a structured, complex and heady wine capable of aging from 5 to 25 years. The alcohol level surpasses 15 to 15.5 percent, with the legal minimum being 14 percent.

Prosecco, a Frizzante (sparkling) white wine made from the Glera grape, is from the northeast of Italy, specifically from the Veneto and Friuli-Venezia Giulia wine regions.

The climate in Veneto is Continental and the ground is composed of volcanic rock and soil.

Tuscany (Toscana)

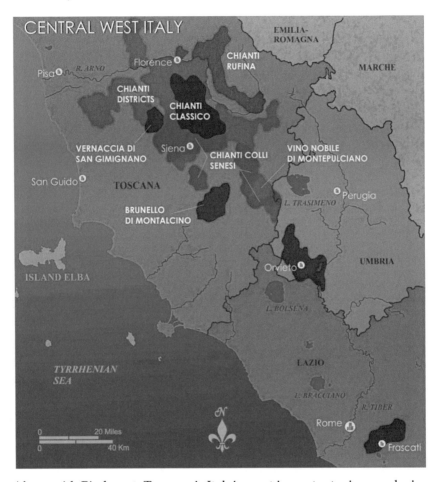

Along with Piedmont, Tuscany is Italy's most important wine-producing area. Chianti, Brunello, Vino Nobile and Vin Santo are known all over the world. Tuscany is also celebrated for its unique Super Tuscan, similar to the Meritage Bordeaux-style in California. Their label, usually Toscana IGP (*Indicazione Geografica y Protetta* meaning Protected Geographical Indication), identifies a product originating from a specific region whose quality and characteristics can be traced back to its geographical origin and of which at least one production and processing phase must take place in the designated zone of production.

I spent a week in Tuscany and Umbria in 1991. I invested a good deal of my time visiting vineyards and wineries in both Montepulciano and Montalcino. It was not nearly enough time in the region, but it was glorious, and I will never forget it. It is also worth mentioning that I enjoyed a delicious three-hour lunch and unique wines in San Gimignano, one of the most interesting walled medieval towns near beautiful Siena. I look forward to revisiting this countryside again soon.

Forty-two grape varieties are grown in Tuscany. Sangiovese is Tuscany's most prominent red grape. Of the many local red grape varieties, Canaiolo, Colorino, Malvasia Nera and

The Town of San Gimignano

Mammolo are the most widely grown. Cabernet Sauvignon, Merlot, Cabernet Franc and Syrah are the international red varieties grown here. Trebbiano is the most widely planted white variety, followed by Vermentino, Vernaccia, Malvasia and Grechetto. Chardonnay and Sauvignon Blanc are the international white grapes.

The climate in Tuscany is Mediterranean, and the soil is marl, sand, silt and clay.

Umbria

Umbria, south of Tuscany in the center of Italy, has many Etruscan ruins and medieval hill towns. Orvieto, Assisi (named after St. Francis of Assisi) and Perugia are wonderful cities to visit and the wines are simply delicious. There are a total of 31 different grape varieties grown in the small region of Umbria. Reds include Sangiovese, Sagrantino, Canaiolo, Trebbiano, Montepulciano, Barbera, Gamay, Merlot, Cabernet Sauvignon and Cabernet Franc. Whites include Grechetto, Trebbiano, Verdello,

Malvasia Bianca, Chardonnay and Sauvignon Blanc. Close to 60 percent of wine produced in Umbria is white. Orvieto accounts for 80 percent of the overall wine production in Umbria. The climate is Mediterranean. Umbria has rich, volcanic *tufo* (chalky clay) soils.

Sicily

Sicily is known for its most famous wine Marsala, which was first made in the city of that name on the western coast in the 1790s. Marsala is produced using the Grillo, Inzolia and Catarratto white grape varieties. Forty grape varieties are grown in this area. Reds include Nero d'Avola, Primitivo, Frappato, Nerello Mascalese and internationals such as Syrah, Cabernet Sauvignon and Merlot. Whites include Malvasia, Zibibbo, Moscato (Muscat), Carricante, Inzolia, Catarratto, Grecanico with some Pinot Grigio and Chardonnay. The climate in Sicily is mild Mediterranean and the soil is volcanic.

Puglia

Puglia (Apulia) forms the 'heel' of Italy's boot-shape. Puglia has always been a large producer of Italian wines because it is free of mountains and consists of mostly flat, fertile plains with a great deal of sunny, dry weather — perfect conditions for grape growing. Puglia has been producing wine for over 2,000 years. Thirty-eight grape varieties are grown in this region. Reds include Negroamaro, Primitivo, Malvasia Nera, Uva di Troia, Montepulciano, Sangiovese, Cinsault, Zinfandel, Ciliegiolo and Aleatico. Of the whites, Bombino Bianco (thought to be related to Trebbiano) is the most planted, followed by Verdeca, Chardonnay, Bianco d'Alessano, Trebbiano Toscano and Malvasia Bianca. The climate in Puglia is Mediterranean with hot and dry summers, mitigated by constant sea breezes. The soil is limestone.

Label Terms

There are six terms used on Italian wine labels. The Vini DOP (Wines with Protected Designation of Origin) category includes two sub-categories which are Vini *Denominazione di Origine Controllate e Garantita* (DOCG) (Controlled and Guaranteed Designation of Origin) and Vini *Denominazione di Origine Controllata* (DOC) (Controlled Designation of Origin). DOCG is the highest ranking of Italian wines. There are strict rules governing the production of DOCG wines, including the permitted grape varieties, yield limits, grape ripeness, winemaking procedures and barrel/bottle maturation. Every DOCG wine is subject to official tasting procedures. To prevent counterfeiting, the bottles have a numbered government seal across the neck label. DOC is the main ranking in the classification of Italian wines. There are approximately 340 individual DOC titles, each with a set of laws governing its viticultural zone, permitted grape varieties and wine style. *Indicazione Geografica Tipica* (IGT), Typical Geographic Indication, is a classification that is foremost recognized for regional wines, rather than grape varieties or wine styles. It is a term that was, in principle, created to recognize the high quality of Super Tuscans. *Vino da Tavola* (VdT) means table wine and represents the most basic level of Italian wine. *Classico* is a geographic term, signifying a traditional zone within the heart of a DOCG area. *Riserva* is a term used for red wines that have aged between 27 and 60 months.

SPAIN

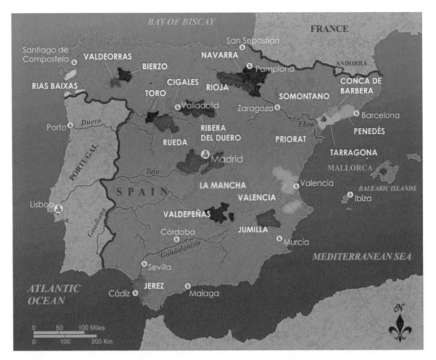

Thanks to the fertile soil, warm climate and tremendous amount of sun, Spain is the third largest producer of wines. With over two million acres, Spain has the most acres of planted vineyards in the world. Diverse regional climates, a unique geography and high altitude make for an impressive variety of wines. Spain is an elevated plateau; little of Spain is at sea level, and while some of the vineyards are flat, many are nearly 3,000 ft (915 m) above sea level. The influence of the Bay of Biscay, Atlantic Ocean and Mediterranean Sea also play a very important role in the ripening of grapes.

Grapes were first cultivated in Spain sometime between 4,000 and 3,000 B.C. under the Romans, who widely traded and exported Spanish wine. The country has an abundance of native grape varieties, with over 400 planted. The white Airén is Spain's most widely planted grape variety; it is found throughout central Spain and for many years has been the base for Spanish brandy. White grapes such as Albarino, Verdejo, Parellada, Viura, Malvasia, Macabeo, Garnacha Blanca and Xarel-lo (grown mainly in Catalan) are also grown here. The red Tempranillo is Spain's second most widely planted grape variety. Other red grape varieties include Garnacha (Grenache), Carinena (Carignan of France), Mazuelo, Graciano and Monastrell (Mourvèdre of France).

I have been fortunate to visit Spain a number of times, both for pleasure and for business. The people are wonderful, the food is *divino*, the regions are breath taking, and the wines offer a multitude of flavor profiles.

The climate is Atlantic, Mediterranean, temperate, hot Continental and semi-arid. Temperatures throughout Spain can fluctuate greatly between 113°F down to -4°F (45°C to -20°C) and annual rainfall averages from 8 to 28 inches (20 to 70 cm) with the exception of Rías Baixas, which gets an annual rainfall between 63 and 71 inches (160 and 180 cm). The average altitude of Spanish vineyards is from sea level to 2,800 ft (850 m).

The soil is limestone, sandy and calcareous clay, chalk, sand, slate and alluvial silt.

Spain has over 65 wine regions and I would love to write about them all; but I have selected the 8 below, since many of the wines from these regions are imported into the United States and Canada and are some of the highest quality wines in the world. Beyond that, I chose to include these particular regions because of their interesting history, notable size or my own personal acquaintance with the area.

That said, don't let your study of Spanish wine regions end with this book. I encourage you to seek out information about Toro, which produces big bold red wines; Jerez where Sherry originates; and Catalonia, where most of Spain's sparkling wine, called Cava, is made.

Rioja

Rioja, established in 1925 and located between the Atlantic and the Mediterranean, is the best known of the Spanish wine regions, with 154,000 acres and over 1,400 wineries. As of 1991, it is one of only two wine regions in Spain to qualify as DOCa, the highest qualification level for a wine region

Vineyards in the Province of La Rioja

according to Spanish wine regulations. (See Label Terms on page 130.) The Cantabria and Demanda mountain ranges and the river Ebro running through the region create various microclimates.

Located partly within the Basque country, Rioja is best known for red wines and the Tempranillo grape (80 percent of which is planted in this region). The versatile nature of this variety means that the region's red wines cover a variety of styles from young, easy-drinking wines to more sophisticated styles capable of many years of cellaring. Though white wines make up only about 10 percent of the wine produced here, some producers do offer rosés and white wines, including some fine, barrel-fermented and oak-aged styles. Viura is the dominant white grape.

A blend of Graciano, Garnacha and Mazuelo grapes may be added to Tempranillo. This gives Rioja wines their distinctive style, especially in barrel-aged wines.

Rioja's first bodegas (wineries) date back to 1870-1890 when French merchants from Bordeaux came to source wine from the region. Throughout the 20th Century, Rioja expanded and established its reputation at home and abroad.

In 2007 Rioja's Consejo Regulador incorporated six additional white grape varieties. They include the local varieties Maturana Blanca, Tempranillo Blanco and Turruntés and three grapes not native to Rioja: Verdejo, Chardonnay and Sauvignon Blanc. The rare red variety Maturana Tinta, rediscovered through research, was also approved by the authorities.

Ribera del Duero

Ribera del Duero is one of my favorite wine regions on earth. I love their high-quality reds, made predominately from the Tempranillo grape, as they are intense, bold and tannic. The region is located north of Madrid and south of Rioja in the middle of northern Spain. Vineyards here are situated to the north and south of the River Duero, which runs from east to west though its middle. The focal point of wine activity is the town of Aranda de Duero, where most of the vineyards are located.

The high altitude of the vineyards is a significant factor where quality is concerned; most are located at 2460 to 2625 ft (750-800 m) above sea level. This means that there is wide variation in temperature, especially during the summer; it is not unusual to reach 95°F/35°C during the day and as low as 54°F/12°C at night in the month of August, which encourages the vines to rest and favors the grapes with a pronounced acidity and concentration.

Viticultural challenges in this area include spring frost, hail and autumn rains.

Ribera del Duero's success is firmly based on Tempranillo (also known locally as Tinto Fino or Tinta del País). The variety is used almost exclusively by producers to make reds with various ageing credentials. While some rosés are also produced, the main focus of the region is high-caliber, oak-aged wines capable of many years of ageing. Winemakers use a combination of American, French and other European oak barrels.

Other red grapes grown here include Cabernet Sauvignon, Merlot, Malbec and Albillo. Garnacha is used for most rosé wines. Albillo is the only white grape grown in this region.

Penedès

The DO (see page 130) of Penedès is where Spain's modern winemaking revolution started. By the 1970s, stainless steel tanks had been adopted and the area began to develop in wine terms with similar dynamism to the nearby city of Barcelona.

The area stretches from the coast to the higher altitudes inland, and it features an array of hillsides, coves and valleys which provide a rich choice of *terroirs* for the viticulturalist and winemaker.

Penedès, established in 1960, is divided into three areas. The lowest, "baix-Penedès", is home to the white Cava grapes Macabeo, Xarello and Parellada. In the middle, "mitja-Penedès", Merlot and Cabernet Sauvignon

Grape Vines Sprouting

are cultivated. The highest "alt-Penedès", with some of the highest vineyards in Europe, is where Chardonnay and other cool climate varieties are grown, as well as the finest Parellada grapes.

White grapes dominate wine production four to one. There has been a slight downward trend in the volumes produced for Macabeo, Xarel-lo and Parellada and an upward tendency for Chardonnay and other white varieties. Red varieties are increasingly favored, especially Cabernet Sauvignon, Tempranillo and Merlot, while the ancient traditional variety Samsó is enjoying a renaissance.

The Consejo Regulador of Penedès has recently introduced the classification "Vino Dulce de Frío", an ice wine equivalent. This natural sweet wine can be made from a wide variety of grapes including Chardonnay, Gewürztraminer, Moscatel varieties and Riesling. Today Penedès boasts over 150 wineries.

Rueda

Located in the heart of Castilla y León northwest of Madrid, Rueda has become a positive addition to Spain's quality white wines. It was granted DO status (see page 130) in 1980 when wine producers demonstrated that when combined with modern winemaking technology (which avoids oxidation), Rueda's cooler climate could produce fresh, fruity white wines based on Verdejo, Sauvignon Blanc and Viura.

Rueda white wines are typically youthful, unoaked and often presented with a screw cap, which reflects the modern approach to winemaking in this region. They can be a blend of all three grapes or made from only one (Verdejo or Sauvignon Blanc). Sauvignon Blanc has been doing very well in the region, and cultivation of Verdejo has increased significantly over recent years and has become a key differentiator in its wines.

In 2001, the DO regulations incorporated red wines, but little red wine is produced in Rueda. Today Rueda has close to 60 wineries.

Priorat

Located in the province of Tarragona and protected by the Sierra de Montsant mountain, Priorat is one of Spain's most acclaimed DO regions, established in 1954. It is also one of its smallest, with 4,760 acres boasting an impressive 90 wineries. It obtained the superior status of DOQ (DOCa) in 2000. (See page 130.)

Priorat burst onto the wine scene in the 1990s after a group of winemakers teamed up to make red wine using low-yielding Garnacha and Cariñena grapes in combination with high-quality grapes such as Cabernet Sauvignon. They were attracted by Priorat's licorella soil, a deep black soil of mineral rich slate, schist and quartz, which imparts minerality, retains adequate water during the ripening period and allows the roots of vines to penetrate deep below the surface. As a result of their efforts, a style of wine appeared that, thanks to local grape varieties, soil and altitude, was distinctive from the local rustic wines being made in Spain at the time. At their best, Priorat wines show incredible concentration and merit bottle ageing to reach their peak.

A Typical Spanish Rural Landscape

More commercial wines from the region, both reds and rosés, often contain some Cabernet Sauvignon, Syrah or Merlot. Some white wines are also made in Priorat and their distinctive local character makes them well worth seeking out.

Navarra

Navarra is located in northeastern Spain and borders the Basque Country, Rioja, Aragón and the Pyrenees. Established in 1933, this wine region was traditionally the source of Spain's rosé wines and some of the country's best rosés are still made here, mainly from the Garnacha grape. Today red wine accounts for at least 75 percent of the region's production. There are approximately 116 wineries in this region.

Navarra encompasses both cooler, mountainous areas and warm, sun-drenched fertile valleys, which significantly influence its wine styles.

Rías Baixas

Hugging the Atlantic Ocean, Galicia is home to pine-lined hills overlooking fjord-like inlets; vines trained on pergolas; and light, fresh, aromatic wines, including the country's most sought-after quality wine: Albariño from the DO of coastal Rías Baixas, established in 1988.

Albariño wines are costly for various reasons. The region's 198 wine producers, known as adegas, tend to be small, and DO regulations permit only bottled wines in order to encourage producers to focus on quality. The size of the vintage can also vary dramatically from year to year due to the damp climate here; note that the average rainfall in this Celtic corner of Spain is far higher than in most other Spanish regions. But the climate does present a major advantage: getting the desired level of acidity for these crisp white wines is rarely a problem for producers in the Rías Baixas.

Most Albariños from the Rías Baixas are unoaked and made to be enjoyed within a year of their vintage.

La Mancha

La Mancha, south of Madrid, at 445,000 acres, is by far Spain's largest DO and one of the largest wine regions in the world. It is also one of the oldest, dating back to the 1930s and is now home to 280 wineries.

Vines are traditionally grown as bush vines. Due to the extreme climate, they are planted at wide intervals, allowing each vine to take as much water from the soil as it needs. Today there are more trellised vineyards and irrigation is allowed, which is a particularly significant development for La Mancha.

There has also been a move towards a wide range of quality-orientated Spanish and international grapes. The white grape Airén still dominates in terms of plantings, along with Macabeo and, increasingly, Chardonnay. But the affordable, easy-to-drink reds (including rosés) and the more sophisticated, aged wines offer the most interest. Tempranillo heads up red wines, along with a number of French grape varieties which have adapted well to the local climate.

Lanzarote Island

The Canary Islands, comprising 10 DO regions, are located far closer to Africa than they are to mainland Spain. Because very little is exported due to strong local demand, the wines from this area are basically unknown to the rest of the world. The climatic conditions, soils and landscapes here have little in common with Spain's DOs. Vineyards typically lie over volcanic bedrock and altitude plays a major role, allowing for greater freshness and acidity in an otherwise humid sub-tropical climate.

One of the DOs, Lanzarote Island, has a very unique soil, as you can see in the photo. Its vineyards are made of black ash lying over black bedrock. Grapes are basically the only fruit cultivated here. Because of the problematic humid wind, each vine is protected by planting it in a hollow surrounded by a mound of stones. The vines are spread out and production is very low. Malvasía is widely planted as well as the local white grape

Licorella Soil

varieties Burrablanca, Breval and Diego. Red, white and rosé wines are produced but Lanzarote is best known for its traditional sweet wines.

Label Terms

There are five label terms used on Spanish wines. *Denominación de Origen-Pago* (DO de Pago) is a designation of the highest standards for outstanding individual single-estates with an international reputation. There are only 15 estates with this status. *Denominación de Origen Calificada* (DOCa), similar to Italy's DOCG designation, is also considered the highest level of Spanish wine classification. DOCa is for regions of consistent quality and is a step above DO level. Only two regions hold DOCa status today: Rioja and Priorat. *Denominación de Origen* (DO) indicates the geographical origin and the style of a wine. To earn the use of a DO title, wines must conform to various production conditions, which apply both to vineyard management and winemaking techniques. Today nearly 70 percent of the total vineyard area in Spain is within the boundaries of a DO region. *Vino de Calidad con Indicación Geográfica* (VC or VCIG) means "Wine of Quality with a Geographical Indication". *Vino de Mesa* (VdM), which means "Table Wine", focuses on the *origins* of the wine, rather than its quality or style.

Ageing Designations

The following designations indicate how long a Spanish wine has spent in the barrel. A wine labeled *Vino Joven* (joven means "young" in Spanish) may not have spent any time in a cask. *Crianza* has been aged for two years; *Reserva* for three years. The *Gran Reserva* designation typically appears in above average vintages with the red wines requiring at least five years of aging.

PORTUGAL

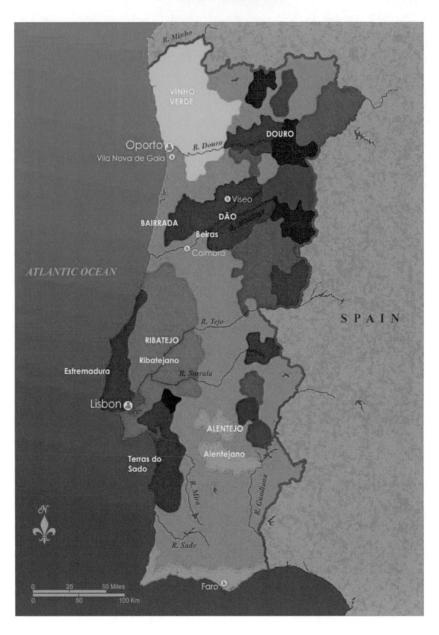

The world's twelfth largest wine producer, Portugal is recognized for its delicious Porto fortified wine, named after Portugal's second largest city, Porto (Oporto). It is also the world's only producer of Vinho Verde, made of Loureiro, Arinto, Trajadura, Avesso and Azal grapes. Portugal started to export its wines to Rome during the time of the Roman Empire.

In the very informative book, *Wine, Andre Domine, 5th Edition*, it is written that there are supposed to be up to 500 grape varieties in Portugal, yet wine experts today have the number estimated at 250 to 300 genuine grape varieties. The two top red varieties are Touriga Nacional and Tinta Roriz (Tempranillo). Also grown are Touriga Franca, Tinta Barroca, Tinto Cão, Tinta Amarela, Baga, Trincadeira, Periquita, Aragonez, Castelao and Jaen. White grape varieties are predominantly Alvarinho, Arinto, Roupeiro, Antao Vaz, Loureiro, Paderna, Bical, Trajadura, Bual, Avesso, Azal and Fernão Pires.

The Atlantic Ocean is a great influence on Portugal, creating a Mediterranean climate with cool, rainy winters and warm summers. Inland the climate is more Continental. The soil is loam, granite and schist.

Portugal has 14 wine-producing regions, two of which, the Douro Wine Region and Pico Island, are protected as World Heritage sites.

Vinho Verde

The Vinho Verde region is found in the North of Portugal. The climate is warm with a great deal of rain in the winter months. The most important grapes are the Loureiro and Paderna. Vinho Verde means "green wine" and refers to the youth of the wine produced there, which should be consumed within one year or so of being bottled. Vinho Verde wines are known for their bright, refreshing and semi-sparkling character, making them perfect for summer drinking. They are typically low in alcohol and cannot exceed 11.5 percent. Vinho Verde wines, which may be red, white or rosé, are the most exported Portuguese wines after Port. Especially in summer months, consider buying a bottle of Vinho Verde and enjoying its refreshing profile.

Vinho Alvarinho is made from Alvarinho grapes, in a small designated sub-region of Monção and Melgaço. These more expensive wines have ripe tropical aromas and higher alcohol levels of 11.5 to 14 percent.

Douro

The Douro region is famous for its gorgeous Port wines. Port is made primarily of Tinta Barroca, Tinta Cão, Tinta Roriz (Tempranillo), Touriga Francesa and Touriga Nacional. The grapes that are not used for Port are blended to make a light wine called Douro. Some excellent red wines are produced having a spicy flavor and full body similar to Port. In the upper parts of

The Douro River

the Douro Valley we are now seeing Cabernet Sauvignon, Sauvignon Blanc and Gewürztraminer. The soil is mostly schist, a bed of rock and mineral. Port is one of my favorite after-dinner drinks and I strongly recommend you give it a taste. For more information on Ports see page 32.

Dao

The Dao region, south of the Douro region, is a mountainous region with a temperate climate. The mountains protect the grapes from maritime and continental influences. The soil is granite and the climate is far more arid. Red wines are made from Jaen, Touriga Nacional and Tinta Roriz grapes; whites from Encruzado grapes.

Bairrada

The Bairrada region is very wet and the soil is clay with limestone. The region is also surrounded by granite-rich hills that shield it from the influence of the Atlantic. The slopes are very steep and vineyards are planted on terraces. By law, red wines produced here must contain at least 30 percent Touriga Nacional grapes. Most wines are blended with at least one other grape variety. Uncommon for Portugal, Bairrada is a region where over 80 percent of wines are red and most of these are made from Baga. White wines are made with the Bical grape. The Bairrada region is better known for its sparkling (Espumante) wine.

Ribatejo

Ribatejo in southern Portugal is known for its wines grown along the banks of the Tagus river. Yields are generally high. White Fernao Pires grapes and red Castelo Frances are prevalent. International grapes such as Cabernet Sauvignon and Merlot have been brought in to offer higher quality wines.

Alentejo

Alentejo is a key wine region in southern Portugal, and some of the best Portuguese wines come from this region. It is also noted for its Corkwood trees where over half the world's supply of cork is grown (see page 45). The climate is continental and the soil is loam, granite and schist. Trincadeira is the most important red grape in the region with Aragonez (Tempranillo) more of a blending grape. Other red grapes include Moreto and Castelao Frances. Whites are made of Roupeiro, Antao Vaz, Perrum and Arinto grapes.

Madeira

The island of Madeira lies in the Atlantic Ocean approximately 300 miles (500 kms) west of Morocco and almost 650 miles (1100 kms) from Lisbon. It is very mountainous with a warm and damp climate. Wine makers here are challenged with fungal disease due to high annual rainfall. The land is very fertile, made of volcanic ash and potash. Interestingly, Madeira wines were historically shipped for long voyages as part of the ageing process. Madeira wines are more often used for cooking than drinking. Grape varieties to make Madeira are Tinga Negra Mole, Sercial, Verdelho, Bual and Malvasia (Malmsey). Three quarters of the vineyards are planted with the Tinga Negra Mole grapes. Madeira wines are described by their sweetness and/or their age.

Label Terms

Portuguese wine regions are grouped into four levels of classification. Top quality wines are labeled *Denominação de Origem Controlada* [Registered Designation of Origin] (DOCs) or *Denominação de Origem Protegida* [Protected Designation of Origin] (DOP). They are "Quality Wines

Produced in Specified Regions" (QWpsr) under the European Union wine regulations. This designation corresponds to the French AOP. Beneath DOC/DOP is *Indicação Geográfica Protegida* [Protected Geographic Indication] (IGP). IGP is a collective designation applicable to wines of a specific region. Next down the quality ladder is *Vinho Regional* (VR) which are regional wines that do not adhere to the same strict regulations as IGP. The lowest quality wine is *Vinho de Mesa*, which is table wine.

Ageing Designations

The term *Reserva* indicates a wine of superior quality that must come from a single vintage. It is a wine of DOC/DOP status. Reds must be aged for at least two years in a cask plus another year in a bottle.

Garrafeira is a term used on wine labels to denote a red wine from an exceptional year that has aged for at least two years in a barrel and one year in a bottle; a white wine must be aged at least six months in a barrel and six months in a bottle. The alcohol level must be at least 0.5 percent higher than the legal minimum for the DOC/DOP region.

GERMANY

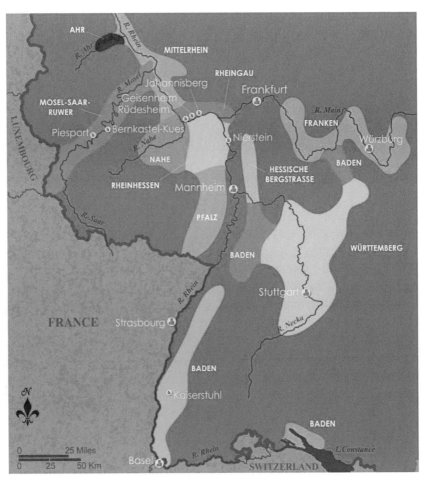

German wines date back to Ancient Roman times between 75 and 275 A.D., and today Germany is the 10th largest producer of wine, with most of its vineyards grown on slopes. The majority of wines are produced in the West along the Rhine River. Some of the world's most northerly wine regions are found in Germany. Germany's wine reputation is primarily based on the Riesling white wine grape variety. *Spätburgunder*, the domestic name for Pinot Noir, is the leading red grape variety. Also grown are the red Blauer Portieser and Dornfelder and the white Müller-Thurgau, Silvaner, Gewürztraminer, Pinot Gris and Kerner .

I am a quarter German and for obvious reasons I very much enjoy this country. The diverse history, old-world towns and delicate nuances of the wines make Germany a very special destination. In 1991, my cousin Chris and I went on a four-day jaunt starting in the Black Forest. Here we tasted more than one lovely wine from the Baden wine region and ate like kings. We then went to Trier, a Roman city that is the oldest city in Germany and enjoyed yet more great whites not far from the Mosel River.

There are three distinct climates in Germany: damp and cool to temperate; sunny and dry to mild; and Continental. The soil is slate, sandstone, shelly limestone, red marl, loess, clay, volcanic, basalt, loam and granite.

There are 13 defined regions known as *Anbaugebiete.* The top six are as follows.

Mosel (Mosel-Saar-Ruwer)

The Mosel-Saar-Ruwer region produces some of the highest quality wines in Germany. The region consists of the two tributaries (Saar and Ruwer) of the Moselle River, and the finest vineyards are found on steeply terraced hills overlooking the river. The best wines are made from Riesling, but increasing amounts of Müller-Thurgau, Elbling and Kerner are being planted.

On the Banks of the Mosel River

Rheingau

Historically, Rheingau produces some of the highest quality wines in Germany. Here, the vineyards have a south-facing view, critical for ripening the grapes in this cold growing region. Riesling is still the primary grape of the region, producing high-quality wines.

Nahe

Nahe is one of the major wine producing areas of Germany, and to many its wines are considered to be as high-quality as those produced in the Mosel and Rheingau Regions. Bad Kreuznach, the wine capital of the region, yields exceptional Riesling wines.

Pfalz

Also referred to as the "Rheinpfalz", Pfalz is one of the *Anbaugebiete* (specified wine regions) of Germany. It is just north of Alsace in France, near the German border, and produces red and white wines of distinction. Pinot Noir from this region is very light in style; Riesling and Müller-Thurgau are the top two white grape varieties

Autumn Harvest

cultivated here. Pfalz is the second largest German region by size and the largest by volume of wine produced.

Rheinhessen

Rheinhessen is Germany's largest wine region. It is bordered by both the Nahe and Rhine rivers. By virtue of its size, the soil and climate in this region are considerably more varied than in those found in Germany's smaller growing zones. Müller-Thurgau is the dominant grape variety, with Riesling being second, followed by Sylvaner.

Ahr

Why is Ahr a unique wine region in Germany? Because of the noted red wine called Spätburgunder, which is produced from the Pinot Noir grapes in this area. Located along the northern Rhine River, the reds have an acidic and slightly spicy, fruity character. Ahr is by far the smallest wine region in Germany.

Label Terms

German wine labels are complex and complicated, yet highly informative. They standardize more information than those of any other nation. A single label may indicate (among other things) the producer's name and location, the wine's sweetness, its grape variety, how ripe the grapes were when harvested, the name of the village and vineyard the grapes came from and whether the wine was bottled at the winery or by a third party. See page 63 for an example of a German wine label.

The VDP (The Association of German Quality and *Prädikat* Wine Estates) is an association of about 200 top German wineries. Membership is voluntary, but requires adherence to strict standards that are well above those required by German wine law. In other words, the VDP is diligently self-administrated. When purchasing German wines look for the VDP eagle symbol, which ensures higher quality.

LEGALLY REQUIRED ITEMS

German wine labels may have up to 13 terms (see page 63), but legally at least 6 items of information must be present on the label. One item is the name of the producer or bottler; another is the location where the wine was produced. The German wine domaines or "châteaux" are often called "*Kloster*", "*Schloss*", "*Burg*", or "*Weingut*", followed by some other name. The A.P.Nr *Amtliche Prüfnummer* quality control number (e.g.: 33050 031 04) is a third. The final two digits denote the year of the testing, which is normally the year following the vintage. They also must list the *Anbaugebiet*, (region of origin), the volume of the wine, the location of the producer/bottler and the alcohol level.

QUALITY CLASSIFICATIONS

German wines are classified for quality as follows. *Qualitätswein mit Pradikat* (QmP) means "quality wine with distinction" and is the top quality wine tier. *Qualitätswein bestimmter Anbaugebiete* (QbA) means "quality wine from a specific region". *Qualitätswein* (Q) means "quality wine". *Landwein* is the German equivalent of *Vin de Pays*. *Deutscher*

Tafelwein (German table wine) is the lowest classification. Only five percent of the wine produced in Germany is table wine.

PRADIKAT LEVEL

The Pradikat (QmP) designation is divided into 6 levels, determined by the ripeness of the grapes at harvest, or the amount of residual sugar in the wine and alcohol level. Kabinett are the most delicate QmP wines. Spätlese is a late harvest wine. Auslese indicates a wine made from individually selected, extra-ripe grapes. Beerenauslese (BA) is a rare, expensive wine from selected grapes suffering from Noble Rot. Eiswein is picked when the temperature is below 14°F/-8°C (similar to Icewine from Canada). *Trockenbeerenauslese* (TBA) means the wine is from a small production of only the finest vintages.

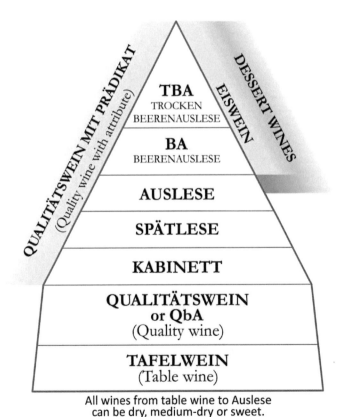

All wines from table wine to Auslese
can be dry, medium-dry or sweet.

German Wine Pyramid

Geographic Classification

Georgraphic classifications on German wine labels include *Einzellage* (an individual vineyard); *Grosslage* (a group of adjoining vineyards); *Gemeind* (a commune); *Bereich* (a district within a region with a number of communes) and *Anbaugebiet* (Designated Quality Region).

CENTRAL AND SOUTHEASTERN EUROPE

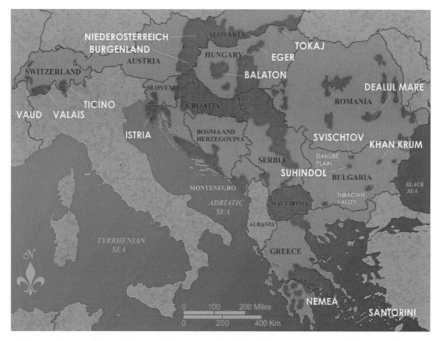

Central and Southeastern Europe offer a multitude of languages, cultures, landscapes, wines and grapes.

Austria

There is archaeological evidence of grapes having been grown in Austria since 6,000 B.C., and today this small country is the 16th largest producer of wine. Austrian wines are mostly dry whites made of Austria's signature grape variety, Grüner Veltliner, which is rather unique in character and not very well known. If you are looking for another white grape variety, give Grüner Veltliner a try. Please see page 24 for additional information regarding its special flavor profile. Other white grapes grown are Riesling and Müller-Thurgau. Approximately 30 percent of the wine is red, made with grapes such as Blaufränkisch, Pinot Noir (Blauburgunder) and Zweigelt. Blauer Portugieser and Gamay are also grown. All producing areas are situated in the East, because the Alps make viniculture unsuitable.

The climate is Central European/Continental with short, cold winters, long warm summers and long autumns. The soil is chalk, gravel, sand, schist, volcanic, limestone and loam.

Austria has four major wine regions, along with twelve smaller ones.

NIEDERÖSTERREICH

Niederösterreich, in the north-east of Austria, is by far the country's largest wine-growing region, with eight specific wine-growing areas. Due to its large geographic size, one sees flat to steep, terraced vineyards. The area of Wachau in this region is stunningly beautiful and is classified as a UNESCO World Heritage site because of its significance as "a riverine landscape bordered by mountains, in which material evidence of its long historical evolution has survived to a remarkable degree" (to quote the UNESCO justification for the honor). Grüner Veltliner is the most widely grown grape of the region, with nearly 45 percent of the area's production. Other grapes are Riesling and Roter Veltliner.

BURGENLAND

Burgenland has four wine areas and is located on the central eastern portion of Austria. Given its latitude, it is somewhat surprising to note that the climate is Continental and hot. Burgenland is known for its full-bodied and rich red wines. It also offers the forward dessert wines, *Trockenbeerenauslese* and *Beerenauslese*. See the

Typical Wine Cellar in Burgenland

German terms in the pyramid on page 141. Though extremely hard to find, if you have the opportunity, try Ruster Ausbruch for a special occasion, as it is comparable to the wonderful dessert wines of Hungary's Tokaji Eszencia or France's Sauternes.

STEIERMARK

Steiermark, also known as Styria, is the southernmost wine-producing region in Austria and one of its smallest. Like Germany and Switzerland, the terrain here is hilly, and many of the vineyards are planted on steep slopes to take advantage of sunlight and winds. The climate has both quasi-Mediterranean and Continental characteristics. The region's specialty is a local rosé called Schilcher which is made from the region's specialty grape, Blauer Wildbacher. Unfortunately, you will rarely see wines from this region, as most of the wines are consumed locally. While three-quarters of the wines are white from Sauvignon Blanc, Chardonnay, Weissburgunder and Welschriesling, there are some delicious red wines made of Pinot Noir and Zweigelt.

WIEN (VIENNA)

Vienna is the only major city in the world that has its own vineyards.

LABEL TERMS

The label terms on Austrian wines are the same as Germany's, with the addition of the term *Ausbruchwein* (*Ausbruch* means "break-out"). You will find the term *Ausbruchwein* on the labels of dessert wines and *Strohweins* (straw wines) made from grapes affected by Noble Rot.

Hungary

Hungary is the world's 20th largest producer and is celebrated for its sweet wines from the Tokaji-Hegyalja region. This region is the second oldest protected wine region in the world, established in 1730. Red grapes grown here are Kekfrankos, Cabernet Franc and Cabernet Sauvignon; whites are Furmint, Hárslevelű, Chardonnay, Irsai Oliver and Pinot Gris. The Hungarian climate is sub-Mediterranean, and the soil is sand, volcanic rock, loess and clay.

Four quality wines with varying levels of residual sugar are produced in Hungary. Tokaji Furming is medium-dry to dry. Tokaji Szamorodni is dry to sweet. Tokaji Aszú is a full-bodied, sweet dessert wine made from grapes affected by botrytis, and in fact the word *aszú* means Noble Rot. Tokaji Aszú matures between three and six years in oak casks; typically wines around the world age in oak for one to two years. Tokaji Eszencia is the world's sweetest wine. Delicious and very expensive, it can be put against a world class Sauternes from France or a Trockenbeerenauslese (TBA) from Germany. It is only made in the very best years, out of grapes from the very best vineyards. If stored properly, Tokaji Eszencia can maintain its quality and drinkability for 100 years or more.

On the Tokaji label, the term *Puttonyus* (Puttonyos in English) indicates the level of sugar, and thus the sweetness, of the Hungarian dessert wine called Tokaji (Tokay in English). Usually, the higher the Puttonyos content, the more expensive the wine. See page 30.

Of the six grapes that are officially approved for Tokaji production (Furmint, Hárslevelű, Yellow Muscat, Zéta [previously called Oremus], Kövérszőlő and Kabar) Furmint is by far the most important. It is used for the production of 60 percent of Aszú wines. The next most important is Hárslevelű, which accounts for another 30 percent. Other white grapes grown in Hungary include Chardonnay, Pinot Gris and Welschriesling.

Hungary has seven wine regions, and by far the best known is Tokaji-Hegyalja.

TOKAJI-HEGYALJA

Tokaji-Hegyalja is a true gem of a place, known for its sweet and thick dessert wine Tokaji Aszú. It is the world's oldest botrytized (Noble Rot) wine.

The Tokaji or Tokaj region has been declared a World Heritage Site. There is no certainty as to when the first wines were produced, but a fair guess would be around the 1100s. In the early 1700s, Tokaji wine was given to King Louis XIV of France, who enjoyed this delicious dessert wine so much he declared it "Wine of Kings, King of Wines". Six grape varieties are officially approved for Tokaji wine production: Furmint which accounts for 60 percent of the region; Hárslevelű, which makes up 30 percent, Yellow Muscat, Zéta, Kövérszőlő and Kabar. With the hope that you like sweet wine, try a bottle of

A Gorgeous Bottle of Tokaji Aszú

Tokaji Eszencia if you can get your hands on one. If not, try the less-expensive Tokaji Aszú.

Because it is sheltered by the Carpathian mountain range, Tokaj's climate is fairly warm. The region's soils include Volcanic clay, loess and sand.

EGER, VILLÁNY AND SZEKSZÁRD

Southern Hungary, especially Villány and Szekszárd, where the climate is mild, produce the best reds. Also notable is the Eger region, which is known for its wine Egri Bikavér, which means "Bull's Blood of Eger". Officially, Egri Bikavér has to contain at least three of a total of thirteen possible grape varieties, Kadarka and Kékfrankos being the two most important. The soils of southern Hungary are volcanic and iron-rich.

LABEL TERMS

Label terms for Hungarian wine are *Különleges Minőséű Bor* for Special Quality Wine (botrysized or Noble Rot wines from grapes known as *Aszú*), *Minőségi Bor*, which means "quality wine" and *Asztali Bor*, meaning "table wine".

Greece

Greece is a breathtaking country offering mountain ranges, the sea, unparalleled history and idyllic islands, as well as an impressive variety of red and white wines. The 15th largest producer, Greece is the oldest wine-growing country in the world, dating back to 8,500 B.C. Greece is known to have about 350 indigenous grape varieties and ranks among the top three countries in the world in terms of the sheer number of grape types planted, along with Italy and Portugal. The best known white wine is the traditional Retsina, flavored with pine resin (traditional appellation). Retsina can be white or rosé and is made of Savatiano or the "Saturday" grape. Today there are a number of delicious dry white and red wines with a variety of distinct characters. The quality of Greek wines has improved dramatically since the 1980s and they may be the most underrated on the planet. It is more than a treat to try new wine varieties from different countries, and Greek wines are an excellent place to start.

The Greek climate is Mediterranean, and the soil is limestone and volcanic.

There are 7 main Greek wine-growing areas with 25 villages where a minimum of 38 grape varieties are primarily grown. Of these regions, the following are the most significant.

MACEDONIA

In Northern Greece (Macedonia), the major appellation is Naoussa made of the red grape Xynomavro. This wine is delicious, offering complex flavors and aromas. The climate is Continental, with cool winters, warm summers and frequent rainfall; the soil is sandy. Most vineyards are cultivated at high altitudes on the Vermio Mountains.

THE PELOPONNESE PENINSULA

One third of Greek wines are produced on the Peloponnese Peninsula. Located in southern Greece, it is separated from the northern part of the country by the Gulf of Corinth. Nemea is the most important AOP region in southern Greece, known for the production of red wines made from the Argiorgitiko grape. The climate is Mediterranean with short, mild winters and hot summers. Because of the intense summer heat, most vineyards are planted at high altitudes, usually above 250 meters.

Santorini Church in a Vineyard

SANTORINI

Among the many Greek islands, Santorini offers the highest quality dry white wines made from the Assyrtiko grape. Santorini is one of the most beautiful islands I have ever visited. The people are very courteous and friendly, and the wine here offers very agreeable characteristics. Because of the constant wind, vines are tied into a basket shape to protect the grapes.

CRETE

Crete is the largest island in Greece, located in the Aegean Sea. It produces the largest volume of wine, of which most is red.

LABEL TERMS

The two label terms used for quality Greek wines are *Onomasia Proelefsis Anoteras Poiotitos* (O.P.A.P.), which means "an Appelation of Origin of Superior Quality" and *Onomasia Proelefsis Eleghomeni* (O.P.E.), meaning a "Controlled Appelation of Origin" usually used for liqueur wines. Other terms seen on lesser quality wines are: *Topikos Oinos* (*Vin de Pays*) and *Epitrapezios Oinos* (*Vin de Table*). Cava is a term for both white and red wines, aged for a minimum of two years for whites and three years for reds. The term Reserve is only used for Appellation of Origin wines. The same applies here as with Cava in terms of aging for whites and reds. The term Grand Reserve can only be used for wines with Appellation of Origin. Whites must be aged for a minimum of three years and reds for a minimum of four years.

GREEK GRAPE VARIETIES

Among the 350 indigenous grapes, there are 7 varieties of Greek grapes that are particularly worth mentioning. Agiorgitiko produces lush, velvety reds with black-cherry flavors. Assyrtiko is used to make minerally, bone-dry, citrus-edged white wines. Wines made from Athiri are characterized by the aroma of stone fruits, like nectarines. Malagousia, a melony, jasmine-scented white grape, was on the brink of extinction before winemaker Evangelos Gerovassiliou began growing it again. Moscofilero is a white grape grown primarily in Peloponnesia. It produces wines with tangerine and blossom scents. Roditis is an elegant and light-bodied, pink-skinned grape used to make crisp whites and rosés. Xinomavro, which means "acid black" in Greek and is named for its dark skin, produces a red wine with floral and spice aromas, firm tannins and vibrant fruit.

Switzerland

Most wines are produced in the western and southern areas of Switzerland along the upper Rhône Valley. It is the 24th largest producer of wines, with most vineyards growing on slopes. Because of Switzerland's varied terrain, numerous microclimates exist. It is known primarily for its dry, unoaked white wine with mineral and distinct earthy flavors, although the country also produces delicious, full-bodied reds. It is one of the most beautiful countries on earth and during one harvest season I had the special fortune of being part of a harvest in the canton, or county, of Vaud. On a cold, drizzly, late October day in 1990 I harvested grapes in the eastern-most part of the canton of Vaud, and I can tell you that it was absolutely breathtaking. Imagine being at a beautiful and storied vineyard, cutting grape stems, loading the grape bunches into large heavy containers and then carrying them down to the building that presses these true jewels. While standing on the very steep slope, you can look below and watch the sun

Grapes Being Cut from Row

glistening on Lake Geneva (also known as Lac Léman). Absolutely magical!

Red grapes grown in Switzerland are Pinot Noir (Blauburgunder), Gamay (wonderful rosés), Merlot and Syrah. White grapes grown here include Chasselas, Müller-Thurgau, Chardonnay, Aligoté, Sylvaner, Pinot Gris, Marsanne, Petit Arvine and Amigne. Switzerland exports less than two percent of its wine and uses the French-style AOP system.

The Swiss climate is temperate; soil is limestone, gravel and schist.

The five most important wine-growing regions in Switzerland include the cantons of Vaud, Valais, Ticino, Geneva and Neuchâtel. Vaud and Valais, which are the most notable, are described below.

VAUD

Vaud, known for its white Chasselas wines, is the second-largest wine region in Switzerland. For one year I lived in the quaint town of Versoix, which is one mile (1.7 km) from the border of the Vaud canton. My home was completely surrounded by vineyards. The main Vaud vineyard area lies along Lake Geneva, which affects the vineyards by reducing the frequency of spring frosts and lowering the temperature in the summer. Vaud produces twice as much white wine as red. While Chasselas is the primarily variety, increasing quantities of Chardonnay, Sauvignon Blanc, Pinot Gris and Viognier are also being grown. The highest-quality red wines produced in Vaud are composed mostly of Pinot Noir and Gamay. The climate is temperate, with a fairly high annual rainfall.

VALAIS

With its bucolic valleys, majestic mountains and steep hillsides, the canton of Valais is one of the most beautiful and impressive winegrowing districts in Switzerland. Vines are grown along 50 miles (80 km) of the Rhône Valley. Some vineyards are on slopes of as much as 70 degrees, and the construction and upkeep of these are extremely labor intensive and very costly. A good deal of wine in this stunning canton is grown at impressively high altitudes; Switzerland boasts some of the highest vineyards in Europe: 2140 ft (650 m) above sea level and some from Haut Valais are grown at 3300 ft (1,000 m). The Valais climate is very dry, with warm summers and cold winters. A wide range of grape varieties is grown here, including some rather rare, indigenous red and white varieties such as: Humagne Blanche and Humagne Rouge, Petite Arvine, Amigne, Cornalin and Heida. Pinot Noir and Chasselas were introduced in the 1800s. Today, Valais offers full-bodied reds from indigenous and international grapes and a number of fresh and earthy whites including Fendants.

Label Terms

Federweisser or Weissherbst is a young, refreshing Pinot Noir bottled from red grapes that were so gently pressed they have the color of white wine. A Schiller wine from Graubünden is a wine made from both red and white grape varieties and appears like a rosé. The well-known Dôle from Wallis is always a blend of at least 85 percent Pinot Noir and Gamay. The Savagnin from canton Waadt is also a blend of Pinot Noir and Gamay. Oeil-de-Perdrix (partridge eye) is a rosé wine made exclusively from the Pinot Noir grape. It is produced in Wallis and Neuchâtel.

AUSTRALIA

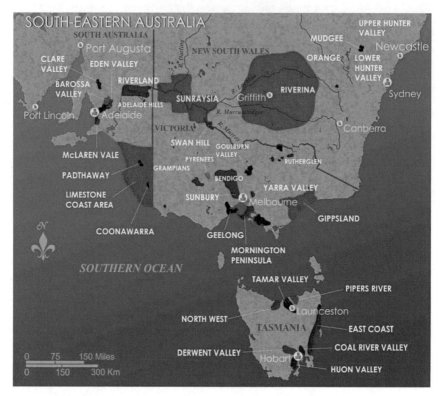

The world's 6th largest wine producer, Australia is home to more than 60 wine regions producing over 100 varieties of grapes, with the top three grapes being Chardonnay, Cabernet Sauvignon and Shiraz (Syrah in France and most of the rest of the world). Most vineyards are found on the lower half of the country's coastline. Australian winemakers creatively blend Shiraz-Cabernet Sauvignon and Chardonnay-Sémillon, making for interesting blended flavor profiles. In fact, taking a cue from Southern Rhône blends, Australia boasts blends of Grenache-Shiraz-Mourvèdre known as GSM blends.

An emerging powerhouse since the mid-1970s, Australian law defines wines by grape varieties, which is easier for U.S. consumers to appreciate. Australia has further developed modern winemaking technologies, enabling the vintners to make both affordable and delicious wines.

The Australian climate is cool and maritime, with wet, humid autumns, but it also has very hot and dry areas. The soil is sandy loam, clay, volcanic earth, limestone and calcareous clay.

Shiraz, Cabernet Sauvignon, Merlot, Pinot Noir, Grenache and Mataro (Mourvèdre) are the red varieties grown here; Chardonnay, Riesling, Sémillon, Sauvignon Blanc, Colombard and Verdelho are the whites. Below are the five most significant wine regions.

New South Wales

New South Wales was the site of Australia's first vineyard and winery, established in the early 1800s. Hunter Valley, in New South Wales, is Australia's oldest wine region. In 1989 I spent a week in Australia and went to Hunter Valley to visit vineyards, tour wineries, taste some wines and eat like a king. Mission was accomplished on all three

Vineyards in Hunter Valley

counts! The state's varying climates has resulted in diverse wine styles including sweet, botrytis-affected white wines. Grapes grown here include Riesling, Sauvignon Blanc and Chardonnay.

Victoria

Leading areas in Victoria are the Yarra Valley and Mornington Peninsula. Victoria is a wonderful wine-producing region thanks to the diversity of its climates. Its warmer climate regions are known for their fortified wine styles, which feature intense fruit flavors. In the cooler maritime climates of the Yarra Valley and Mornington Peninsula, you'll find crisp Chardonnays and complex Pinot Noirs.

South Australia

Key areas in South Australia include renowned Barossa, Adelaide Hills, Clare Valley, Coonawarra and McLaren Vale. More than half of Australia's wines are produced in South Australia, making it the wine capital of the nation. The Barossa Region is home to some of the world's best Shiraz, along with Cabernet Sauvignon and Merlot.

Vineyards in McLaren Vale

You will find outstanding Rieslings from Eden Valley. Because of the cool climate and high precipitation in Adelaide Hills, Pinot Noir, Chardonnay and Sauvignon Blanc produce some outstanding wines. Clare Valley is famous for its Riesling.

Western Australia

The best known wine area in Western Australia is Margaret River, which has an international reputation for fine wines made of Cabernet Sauvignon and Chardonnay. Other grape varieties produced here include Sauvignon Blanc, Sémillon and Shiraz.

Tasmania

Tasmania, an island off the southern tip of Australia, has seven wine-growing areas. Due to its cool climate, Tasmania produces mainly Chardonnay and Pinot Noir and their wines are becoming more popular throughout the world.

Label Terms

An important labeling law in Australia revolves around the regional classification of wine-producing areas, known as Geographical Indications or GIs. Its aim is both to indicate the wine's origin and protect a region's name. For a wine to bear a GI name on its label, 85 percent of the grapes in that wine must come from a single vintage, grape variety or region.

It is interesting to note that as of 2002, both Australia and New Zealand now require that allergen warnings appear on their wine labels, because both egg whites and milk are used to refine and clarify their wines.

NEW ZEALAND

New Zealand is the 14ᵗʰ largest wine producer with eleven wine-growing regions extending 990 miles (1,600 km); six on the North Island and five on the South Island. The very first grapes were planted in 1819. The Catholic Marist brothers, from France, made wine for church rituals in the 1850s. Chardonnay, Sauvignon Blanc and Pinot Noir account for close to 70 percent of vineyards in New Zealand, which produces some of the very best Sauvignon Blanc wines, and they seem to be improving every year. The best known wines come from Gisborne, Hawke's Bay and Marlborough.

The climate on North Island is Maritime and subtropical; with very fertile, heavy clay soils. On South Island the climate is Continental, with stony soil.

Red grape varieties grown here are Pinot Noir, Syrah, Cabernet Sauvignon, Petit Verdot, some Cabernet Franc and Malbec. White Grape Varieties are Chardonnay, Sauvignon Blanc, Riesling, Pinot Gris and Müller-Thurgau.

North Island

GISBORNE

Gisborne is New Zealand's fourth largest grape-growing region. It is the first wine region in the world to see each new day's sun. Gisborne is the Chardonnay capital of New Zealand and other widely planted white grape varieties include Chenin Blanc and Gewürztraminer. Gisborne is exposed to cyclones, creating significant variations in quality from year to year. Soil is very fertile and tends toward alluvial loams on sandy or volcanic subsoils.

HAWKE'S BAY

Hawke's Bay is New Zealand's second largest wine-growing region. A great deal of sun and a variety of soil types make Hawke's Bay very well suited for growing grapes. Chardonnay is the most widely planted grape variety, but a long ripening season allows the growing of red grape varieties such as Cabernet Sauvignon, Merlot, Cabernet Franc and Syrah. Soil is mostly Gimblett gravel.

MARTINBOROUGH

Martinborough sits at the foot of New Zealand's North Island. It is a small wine area with a large number of vineyards producing primarily Pinot Noir. Less than two percent of the country's wine production takes place here. Other varieties include Riesling, Syrah and Pinot Gris. Martinborough has a warm microclimate with hills to the east and west. Almost all the vineyards are thin strips of land on the Dry River to the south. Because these vineyards follow dry riverbeds the soils are layers of alluvial river terraces and silty river loam over stony sub-soils.

South Island

MARLBOROUGH

Located at the top of the South Island, Marlborough is New Zealand's largest wine-growing region. It is said to produce the best Sauvignon Blanc in the world. High quality Chardonnay, Riesling and Pinot Noir are also produced here. Marlborough accounts for approximately two thirds of New Zealand's wine plantings, of which Sauvignon Blanc vines dominate. The climate is close to perfect with its many days of sun, cool nights, minimal autumn rains and alluvial soils combining to make Marlborough one of the world's great wine-producing regions.

NELSON

Nelson is one of the country's smallest wine regions. Nelson vineyards concentrate on grape varieties suited to cooler conditions such as Chardonnay, Sauvignon Blanc, Riesling and Pinot Noir. Abundant sun, fertile plains and snowcapped mountain ranges make it an excellent region to grow grapes. Soil is clay loam over a hard clay subsoil.

CANTERBURY/WAIPARA

Canterbury is located on the East Coast of the South Island. Though a relatively new wine region (1970s) it is becoming well known for its Riesling and Pinot Noir wines. The soils of the region are stony and alluvial. The climate is hot and dry in the summer with cool, clear winters and the possibility of frost. Waipara is quickly becoming internationally known for its high-quality Riesling wines. Soil is gravel and clay.

CENTRAL OTAGO

Central Otago lies on the shores of Lake Wakitipu and is surrounded by the snowcapped Southern Alps, where Queenstown is at the center of the region. Central Otago is the world's southernmost wine producing region and New Zealand's only region with a Continental

Otago Vineyard at Sunset

climate. The summers are hot and dry; the winters are crisp with light snow. Some of New Zealand's very best Pinot Noir wines are produced in this region. Soil structures are heavy mineral deposits in silt loams.

Label Terms

For a wine to be labeled as a single variety, vintage or area, at least 85 percent of the grapes used in that wine must be from that stated variety, vintage or area. Similarly, at least 85 percent of the grapes used in blends must be of the stated varieties, vintages or areas.

SOUTH AFRICA

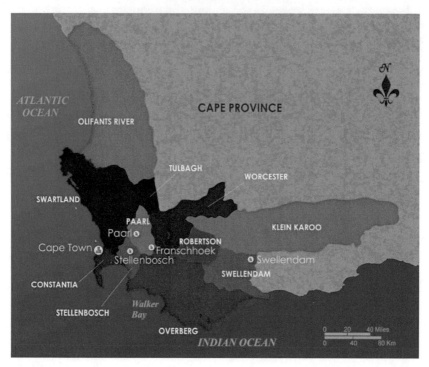

The Atlantic and Indian Oceans influence South Africa's climate along the coast, affecting vine growth. It is the world's 8th largest producer of wine, with Pinotage as the signature grape variety. South Africa's wine roots can be traced as far back as the Dutch colonists, who first planted vines in South Africa in the 1650s. With the arrival of the French Huguenots and their viticultural skills and knowledge in the 1680s, wine production in South Africa was taken to new heights.

South African wine-producing regions have a Mediterranean climate. Influenced by the meeting of the Atlantic and Indian Oceans, they experience a great deal of sun and dry heat. The soil here is granite, iron-rich clay and sand.

Cinsaut (spelled without the "l" in South Africa) is the most common red grape variety grown in South Africa. Pinotage, created in Stellenbosch, South Africa in 1925, is a cross between Pinot Noir and Cinsaut. If you are looking for a change from your Cabernet Sauvignon, try Pinotage—I promise you will be pleasantly surprised. Other important red grapes

160

grown here are Cabernet Sauvignon, Shiraz and Merlot. Whites grown in South Africa are Chenin Blanc (known as Steen), Colombard, Sauvignon Blanc, Chardonnay and, to a small extent, Viognier.

Under the Wine of Origins legislation, wine regions in South Africa are divided into 4 classifications: geographical units, regions, districts and wards. Regions are the largest vineyards; there are five regions in South Africa. Districts are groups of wards, of which there are 16. Wards are a collection of estates, the approximate equivalent of a European appellation. There are approximately 50 wards in South Africa. The best wines are produced in the regions of Constantia, Stellenbosch and Paarl. Overberg is a well-known district in the Cape South Coast Region.

Vineyards in Stellenbosch

Constantia

On the outskirts of Cape Town is Constantia, the oldest district of the region, with several top-notch vineyards that are planted on the slopes of Constantia Mountain, where they are cooled by the sea breezes. The nearby South Atlantic Ocean offers perfect conditions for Sauvignon Blanc and Sémillon grapes. The delicious sweet wines of Constantia are made of Muscat Blanc à Petits Grains, Muscat of Alexandria (Hanepoort) and Pontac.

Stellenbosch

Stellenbosch is further inland where it is warmer and the soil is of sandstone and granite. It is best recognized for its signature Pinotage and Bordeaux blends made with Cabernet Sauvignon and Merlot. Stellenbosch is considered by many to be the finest wine area in South Africa, especially for reds. The landscape is very diverse from sea-facing slopes to valley-hugging hills. Chenin Blanc also does very well in this region.

Paarl

The Paarl region, north-west of Cape Town, was traditionally a white wine region but given its Mediterranean climate and *terroirs* it is today more focused on red wines. As Paarl is warmer than Stellenbosch, the very best wines come from the more elevated vineyards. Winemakers today are concentrating on Syrah, Pinotage, Cabernet Sauvignon, Chenin Blanc and, to a lesser extent, Viognier and Mourvèdre.

Overberg

In the district of Overberg you will find the ward of Walker Bay, where some of the country's best Chardonnays and Pinot Noirs are produced. Syrah is becoming a more important grape variety in the region. Two well-known wine towns of Walker Bay are Worcester and Robertson. Worcester and its surrounding areas comprise just over 20 percent of South Africa's vineyards.

Label Terms

South African labeling law focuses on geographical origins and falls under the purview of the "Wine of Origin" (WO) legislation. Under its certification process, vintage dated wine must be composed of at least 85 percent grapes that were harvested that vintage year. Varietal wines must also be composed of at least 85 percent of the listed variety to be approved for the export market. A wine can be designated as originating from a single vineyard as long as that vineyard is registered with the government, and 100 percent of the grapes used to produce the wine were grown in that vineyard. While the term "estate" is no longer a valid designation under the WO system, wines can be labeled as an "estate wine" if all the grapes were grown and the wine was produced and bottled on the property.

SOUTH AMERICA

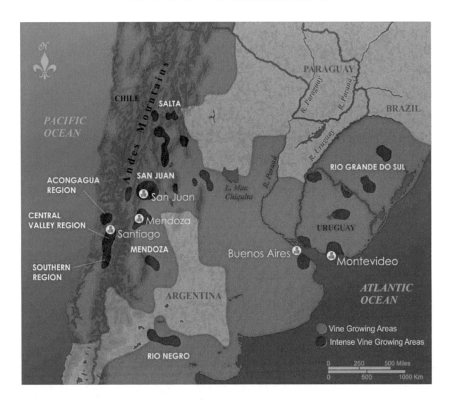

Argentina

Argentina is the fifth largest wine producer in the world and the largest in South America. From north to south, it extends 2,270 miles (3,650 km). Argentina is located on the east side of the Andes mountain range. The valleys in and along the foothills of the Andes Mountains provide ideal conditions for growing vines. Wine production was first introduced to Argentina during the Spanish colonization of the Americas and then by Christian missionaries. In the late 1550s, a Catholic father established the first vineyard in San Juan and Mendoza wine regions of Argentina with cuttings from the Chilean Central Valley. Argentina's winemaking regions are located within an arid (hot, dry and sunny) desert climate. Most vineyards lie at 1,640 ft (500 m) above sea level, and water for irrigation is provided by ample snowmelt coming off the Andes. The combination of warm sunny days and frequent cool nights creates a favorable environment for exceptional grape growing, although, due to the Andes, temperatures can fluctuate up to 50°F/10°C within a single day, and hail is a regular concern. The vineyards of Argentina rarely have to contend with insects, fungi or molds, because of the high altitude and low humidity, so little to no pesticides are required to protect the vineyards. The soil is clay and sand.

Argentina has two signature grape varieties. One of them is the red Malbec, which has recently surpassed Bonarda as the most widely planted wine grape in Argentina. Malbec is Argentina's best known red wine, and the best quality Malbec wines come from the high altitude wine regions of Mendoza. Bonarda has been used for bulk production of table wines with some exceptions. Other red varieties now include Cabernet Sauvignon, Merlot and Syrah.

Argentina's second signature grape variety is the white grape Torrontés, and it is one of the only countries in the world that produces this variety. The most significant varieties are: Torrontés Sanjuanino, Torrontés Mendocino and Torrontés Riojano. Torrontés Riojano is the most widely planted of the three and typically produces better-quality wines. Other white grapes grown here include Chardonnay, Sauvignon Blanc and Viognier.

CENTRAL-WEST REGION

This region is comprised of vineyards located in the provinces of Mendoza and San Juan and accounts for over 90 percent of Argentina's wine production, 60 percent of which is produced in Mendoza. Mendoza is also the only wine-growing region with a hierarchy of appellations. Altitudes range between 1,900 and 2,300 ft (580 and 700 m) above sea level. Annual rainfall is less than 8 inches, but abundant snow in the mountains allows for irrigation when required. The region is well-suited to the production of white wines such as Chardonnay, Sauvignon Blanc, Chenin Blanc, Ugni Blanc and Torrontés. Reds like Cabernet Sauvignon, Malbec,

Volcano Aconcagua and Vineyard

Syrah and Bonarda are grown in the Upper Mendoza River. Soil is calcareous and sand.

San Juan province is the second most important wine-producing region, where the climate is considerably hotter. Here approximately 25 percent of Argentina's wines are produced. The climate is warm and sunny most of the year (around 330 days of sun). San Juan has a cultivated area standing between 2,000 and 4,600 ft (610 to 1,400 m) above sea level with annual rainfall of four inches. Red Syrah, Malbec, Cabernet Sauvignon, and Bonarda and the whites Chardonnay and Torrontés are the most widely cultivated grape varieties. Soil is sandy.

The cooler sub-region Uco Valley features vineyards at more than 5,600 ft (1,710 m) above sea level. In this area you will find white wines such as Chardonnay and Sémillon. Reds from this area such as Malbec, Merlot and Pinot Noir have great aging capacity.

NORTHWEST REGION

This area encompasses the provinces of Salta and La Rioja. The vineyards account for about four percent of Argentina's total wine production. In La Rioja province, where it is still hotter, exported wines are labeled Famatina Valley to avoid confusion with Spain's Rioja wines. The highest vineyards are 5,640 ft (1,720 m) above sea level. The climate is characterized by wide variations in temperature, long summers and low rainfall. The main varieties are white Torrontés Riojano grapes, the typical variety of the region. Red varieties are less extensively grown and include Bonarda and Syrah.

Cafayate in the Northern Salta province is where you will find the white Torrontés Riojano grape, the red Malbec, Cabernet Sauvignon and Tannat. The grape-growing area starts at an altitude of 4,900 ft (1,495 m) above sea level and incredibly reaches 10,210 ft (3,000 m) high, which makes this area the highest grape-growing region in the world. Due to the high altitude, the climate is cool with eight inches of rain per year. The dry, desert-like conditions and significant daily temperature shifts help bring out the best in Torrontés.

SOUTH REGION

In Patagonia lie some of the world's most southerly vineyards. Standing at an altitude of 1,400 ft (430 m) above sea level, the High Valley of Río Negro has a dry, continental climate, with an annual rainfall of less than eight inches and very low relative humidity. Winters are cold and summers warm and dry, with abundant sunshine. The Río Negro region produces Malbec, Sauvignon Blanc, Sémillon, Merlot and Pinot Noir. Soil is sandy.

LABEL TERMS

There are three levels of wine quality based on geographic specificity: *Denominacion de Origen Controlada* [Appellation of Origin] (DOC), for wines meeting stricter requirements regarding the region, climate, and grape varieties; *Indicación Geográfica* [Geographical Indication] (IG), wines vinified and bottled in a designated area; and *Indicación de Procedencia* [Indication of Provenance] (IP), which requires that 80 percent of the grapes in the wine come from the IP region.

Chile

The world's 9th largest producer of wines, Chile is a long, narrow country that is climatically affected by the Andes on its east and the Pacific Ocean on its west. Chile stretches over 2,670 miles (4,300 km) from north to south, but only 210 miles (350 km) at its widest point east to west. Due to its length, Chile has a remarkable variety of climates and landscapes. The winegrowing area is approximately 800 miles (245 km) long and 95 miles (30 km) wide.

Vineyards of Chile

Chile has a very old viticultural history dating back to the 16th century when the Spanish conquistadores and missionaries brought vines from Europe. Today there are over 75 wine producers. Chile is also known for its Pisco brandy.

The Chilean Maritime climate is close to perfect, hot with cooling winds from the Pacific, and altitudes are considerable—think Andes. Chile has very long ripening seasons. Soil is very fertile and composed of limestone-clay, alluvial silt and volcanic rock. Reds grown here include Cabernet Sauvignon, Merlot, Carménère and, more recently, Pinot Noir, Syrah and Malbec. Whites include Chardonnay, Sauvignon Blanc and of late Riesling and Gewürztraminer, due to the cool climate in parts of Chile.

Vineyard regions in Chile are divided into subregions, the subregions into zones, and the zones into areas. There are many regions where fine wines are produced in Chile, but we will focus on the three which are the major exporters of this country.

INLAND VALLEYS REGION

Most vineyards in the Inland Valleys Region lie near the Pacific Ocean, where the cold Humboldt current creates a Maritime climate. Over 85 percent of exported Chilean wine is produced in the Inland Valleys Region. The Maipo Valley subregion, where old Cabernet Sauvignon vines are grown, is known for its fine red wines. Soil is sandy and gravel to the East with more clay to the West. In the Rapel Valley subregion is the Colchaqua Valley zone where delicious wines are made of Cabernet Sauvignon, Carménère and Merlot varieties.

Soil is clay, sand and granite. Another subregion to note is Curicó, where more than 30 varieties of wine grapes have been cultivated since the mid-1800s.

ACONCAGUA REGION

The primary feature of the Aconcagua Region is Mt. Aconcagua, whose towering, snowy peaks provide water to the valley below. While red grapes have long been grown in the interior of this region, we are now beginning to see coastal plantations of white grapes. The best Chilean Chardonnay, Sauvignon Blanc and Pinot Noir come from the Casablanca Valley. This is due to its proximity to the Atlantic Ocean. The climate is cool with morning fog slowing down the ripening of the grapes; a longer time on the vine allows the development of complex flavors. Cabernet Sauvignon, Syrah and Carménère are grown as well. Soil is clay and sandy to the east and granite and clay to the west.

SOUTHERN VALLEY REGION

The sub-region of Bío-Bío also enjoys a long ripening season, but the high rainfall, strong winds and greater extremes of this area make for much more challenging growing conditions. Pinot Noir, Chardonnay, Sauvignon Blanc and Riesling are primarily cultivated. Soils are alluvial, clay and sand.

The sub-region Itala is known for its Cabernet Sauvignon, Merlot, Chardonnay and Gewürztraminer grapes. Some of the earliest vineyards were planted during colonial times. The climate is Mediterranean with slightly less rainfall than Bío-Bío. The soils are alluvial, clay and sand.

LABEL TERMS

Chile's wine laws are similar to the U.S. appellation system. To be exported, the wine must contain 85 percent of the variety listed on the label, as well as at least 85 percent from the designated vintage year. To list a particular wine region, 85 percent is also the minimum requirement of grapes that need to be from that given region. The term *Reserve* has no legal definition.

Uruguay

Located on the Atlantic coast below Brazil and east of Argentina, Uruguay is the 23rd top producer of wine in the world and the fourth largest in South America. The wine industry in Uruguay dates back to the 1870s and was introduced primarily by Basque and Italian immigrants. It is a rather unknown wine-producing country, but today they are making far better wines thanks, in large part, to the improvement of winemaking technologies. I have included Uruguay because I recommend trying, at least once, a wine made of Tannat grapes. Just as Chile is known for Carménère and Argentina for Malbec and Torrontés, Tannat, originally from the southwest of France, has become Uruguay's signature grape variety. Other red grapes grown in Uruguay include Merlot, Cabernet Sauvignon and Cabernet Franc. Muscat Hamburg is grown to create rosés and white grapes include Chardonnay, Pinot Blanc and Sauvignon Blanc.

The climate in Uruguay is temperate, similar to that of Bordeaux, with an average temperature of 66°F/18°C. Rain is consistent throughout the year. The soil is heavy clay and sand. Wines from Tannat are best consumed in four to twelve years.

Most of the vineyards of Uruguay are located in the hills north of the capital, Montevideo. Its top-producing departments include Canelones, Montevideo and San José.

LABEL TERMS

Wines from Uruguay use the following terms, in order from highest to lowest quality: *Vino de Calidad Preferente* (VCP), which means "Preferred Quality Wine" and *Vino Común* (VC) which means "Common or Table Wine".

TOP 20 WINE PRODUCTION BY COUNTRY, 2014

Wine is the most civilized thing in the world.
Ernest Hemingway

Sixty-six countries in the world produce wine. France and Italy make up over 30 percent of world wine production, Spain and the United States over 23 percent, and the top ten producers combined account for over 80 percent. The fastest growing wine-producing countries in the world are Chile, Australia, South Africa and China.

The chart that follows shows the top 20 wine-producing countries, along with their production by the liter.

Rank	Country	Production (Liters 000)
1	France	4,615,100
2	Italy	4,442,400
3	Spain	3,700,000
4	United States	2,250,000
5	Argentina	1,520,000
6	Australia	1,256,000
7	China	1,178,000
8	South Africa	1,142,000
9	Chile	1,003,000
10	Germany	972,500
11	Russia	600,000
12	Portugal	588,600
13	Romania	409,300
14	New Zealand	320,000
15	Greece	290,000
16	Austria	281,000
17	Brazil	243,000
18	Serbia	231,000
19	Ukraine	210,000
20	Hungary	180,000

Note that France and Italy regularly swap positions as the world's top wine producer. Though China is ranked 7th and Russia 11th, I have not included them in *My Wine Guide (made simple)* because we see very little wine imported from either of these markets into the United States and Canada. The same applies to the wines of Romania, Brazil, Serbia and the Ukraine.

THE VERY BEST VINTAGES SINCE 1945

I often wonder what the Vintners buy one half so precious as the goods they sell.
Omar Khayya

This chapter lists the very best vintages, by country or region, since 1945. These are the years which, due to a combination of factors such as weather and soil, and according to wine experts, have produced the very best wine.

Bordeaux Reds	1945*, 1947, 1949, 1953, 1959, 1961*, 1962, 1982, 1985, 1986, 1989, 1990, 2000, 2005, 2009, 2010
Sauternes	1945, 1953, 1961, 1986, 1988, 1989, 1990, 2001, 2005, 2007, 2009
Burgundy Reds	1945, 1949, 1959, 1962, 1969, 1978, 1985, 1988, 1990, 1999, 2002, 2005, 2009, 2010

Burgundy Whites	1947, 1962, 1966, 1985, 1986, 1989, 1996, 2002, 2005, 2009, 2010
Champagne	1964, 1971, 1975, 1976, 1979, 1982, 1985, 1988, 1990, 1996, 2002, 2004, 2005, 2008, 2009
Rhône Reds	1953, 1970, 1972, 1978, 1989, 1990, 1998, 1999, 2000, 2003, 2005, 2009
Italian Barolo	1953, 1971, 1978, 1982, 1989, 1990, 1996, 2001, 2004, 2006, 2007, 2009
Spain Reds	1953, 1962, 1974, 1983, 1990, 2001, 2004, 2005, 2010
Germany	1953, 1971, 1973, 1990, 2004, 2005, 2006, 2007
Ports	1963, 1970, 1977, 1992, 2005, 2008, 2009, 2010
California Reds	1970, 1974, 1976, 1978, 1986, 1987, 1991, 2002, 2003, 2005, 2007, 2009, 2010
Australia Reds	1976, 1986, 1990, 1991, 1998, 2002, 2005, 2006, 2009, 2010
Amarone	1983, 9188, 1990, 1995, 1997, 1998, 2000, 2004, 2006, 2009, 2012

* 1945 and 1961 are considered by many experts to be the "century vintages" of Bordeaux.

TALKING WINE

WINE

PART IV

DINNER CONVERSATION

If food is the body of good living, wine is its soul.
Clifton Fadiman

If you are interested in wine-related trivia, consider entertaining your dinner guests with the following.

Cost

What is in the cost of a bottle of wine? The bottle itself, the front and back labels, the collar/foil, the cork or twist cap and finally the wine all contribute to the price that you pay. All are essentially standard, except for the most important component: the juice. This means that the cost of the bottle, labels, collar/foil and cork or twist cap are pretty much the same whether you are buying a $10 bottle of wine or a $50 bottle of wine.

The lower the price of the bottle of wine, the greater will be the proportionate cost of the glass bottle, labels, cork and foil. Paying merely a few dollars extra for a bottle of wine can mean an exponential difference in the quality of what is in the bottle, because the cost disparity reflects a variation in the quality of the wine *only* and has nothing to do with how it is packaged. The only exception to this is when you are purchasing extremely expensive wines. Very fine wines use slightly longer and better quality corks, which are more expensive than the standard corks discussed above.

Bottle Shapes

People often ask me about shapes of wine bottles. The bottle on the left is a Burgundy, the slender bottle in the middle is from Germany and Alsace, France, and the bottle on the right, with shoulders, is from Bordeaux.

Alcohol Content

Alcohol levels in wines are logarithmic. A wine with 11 percent alcohol is not one percent stronger than a wine with ten percent alcohol. It is in fact ten percent stronger, so the difference is substantial.

Wine and Health

> *Wine from long habit has become an indispensable for my health.*
> Thomas Jefferson

Studies have shown over and over again that moderate consumption of wine helps consumers live longer and suffer from fewer diseases of the heart than heavy drinkers or teetotalers. Moderate drinking is one or two glasses a day.

One glass = four ounces = 100 calories @ 12.5 percent alcohol.

Asthmatics and diabetics must pay close attention to the consumption of wine due to its alcohol, sugar and sulfites. Otherwise, enjoy your wine—and the world of wines—in moderation.

My son Christopher took a course called "World of Chemistry: Food" taught by Professor Fenster at McGill University, and below is a short section from the course that I think you will find interesting.

The health benefits of red wine have been widely discussed, especially in reference to the "French Paradox" and the Mediterranean diet. While the French generally smoke more and eat a diet with higher concentrations of saturated fats than North Americans, the incidence of heart disease in much of France is lower. Studies are inconclusive on whether the consumption of red wine contributes to this difference or if it is rather a side effect of other lifestyle and socio-economic patterns.

One glass of wine (4 oz. = 100 cal. at 12.5 percent alcohol) does contain some vitamins, but you would have to drink *ten* bottles a day to reach your recommended daily allowance (RDA). Resveratrol and flavonoids are also found in wine to varying degrees, and these two antioxidants have been proven to prolong life in lab rats. A human would have to drink 1,500 bottles a day to simulate the levels of resveratrol consumption in the study, however I would strongly discourage you from doing so.

FAVORITE WINE QUOTES

I will drink no wine before its time. It's time.
Benjamin Franklin

I love the English language and read a great deal of its history, etymology, slang and quotes. Below are a few that I enjoy pertaining to wine—some are funny, others profound. The first is my favorite by far.

May friendship, like wine, improve as time advances and may we always have old wine, old friends and young cares.
Anonymous

The best audience is intelligent, well-educated and a little drunk.
Alben W. Barkley

Wine is the intellectual part of a meal, meats are the material part.
Alexandre Dumas

*The definition of true civility is a glass of Champagne at 6:00 o'clock
each and every evening.*
Anonymous, with slight editing by the author

*Wine stimulates the appetite and enhances food. It promotes
conversation and euphoria and can turn a mere meal into a
memorable occasion.*
Derek Cooper

*No man has the right to inflict the torture of bad wine upon his
fellow creatures.*
Marcus Clarke

When wine enlivens the heart, may friendship surround the table.
Anonymous

*A bottle of wine contains more philosophy than all the books in the
world.*
Louis Pasteur

*It's a privilege to drink good wine. We should treat it with respect
and savor every drop, like experts.*
Ralph Steadman

Bacchus opens the gates of the heart.
Horace

Wine is earth's answer to the sun.
Margaret Fuller

The taste of good wine is remembered long after the price is forgotten.
Hubrecht Duijker

I feast on wine and bread, and feasts they are.
Michelangelo

In victory you deserve Champagne, in defeat, you need it.
Napoleon

A bottle of wine begs to be shared; I have never met a miserly wine lover.
Clifton Fadiman

Wine was created from the beginning to make men joyful, not to make them drunk.
Ecclesiastes 31

GLOSSARY OF WINE TERMS

I had to cook a dinner glorious enough to complement the Lafite. It took four days...
Gael Green

ACIDIC/ACIDITY

This is essential to the balance of all wines. It gives zest and freshness. Too much can make wine taste like lemon. The presence of acid is necessary for wine to age and gives it a lively, crisp quality. Acid is tasted on the sides of the tongue and mouth.

AERATE

To allow a wine to "breathe" by exposing it to oxygen. Aerating a wine helps it to mellow and develop its full flavors, especially red wines. Decanting is a way to aerate wine. Young wine that has not been aerated can taste bitter and have a strong taste of alcohol. NOTE: The older the wine, the less it needs aerating as old wines tend to fade much more quickly than younger ones.

ALCOHOLIC

A wine out of balance with too much alcohol. This is a pet peeve of mine: a throat burning red wine with too much alcohol and not nearly enough off-setting flavor. I also call this type of wine "hot".

ANIMAL

The note one might get when smelling or tasting a big robust red. Also known as having a "barnyard" quality.

APPELLATION

A specific geographical area from which a wine is produced. Most European wines are named by appellation rather than grape variety. U.S. wines are named after grape varieties.

AROMA

The smell of wine. There are an unlimited number of aromas in wine and just as many descriptive adjectives for those aromas. True wine appreciation will allow you to decipher and describe those aromas for yourself.

ASTRINGENT/ASTRINGENCY

A mouth-puckering sensation caused by the acid and tannin in a wine. Astringency often declines as a wine ages. Think of the taste of legumes, raw fruits and vegetables. A perfect example of astringency is chewing on cranberries.

BALANCE

Harmony among the wine's components: acid, alcohol, fruit/sweetness and tannins. When a wine tastes and feels balanced in the mouth none of the wine's components will stand out above the other. See **elegant** and **smooth**.

BIG

One of the terms used to describe a "full-bodied" wine with plenty of flavor. A big wine has a powerful aroma with high alcohol, tannins and flavor.

BODY

The texture and weight of a wine. The taster feels the chemical compound glycerin as body, but alcohol content and fullness of flavor also contribute to the feeling of weight in the mouth.

BOTRYTIS CINEREA

Fungus that attacks the grape. It may cause unwanted gray rot or desirable Noble Rot. See **Noble Rot**.

BOUQUET

All the aromas in a wine collectively, when smelling and tasting, make up its bouquet.

BREATHE

To aerate or to allow air to mix with the wine. Key: The older the vintage the less it needs to be aerated. See **aerate**.

CAPSULE/COLLAR/FOIL

The protective foil that covers the cork at the neck of the bottle. This foil sleeve protects the cork from pests such as rats or cork weevils during storage and serves as a decorative collar to catch small drips when pouring. Winemakers historically used capsules of lead,  but as this may leave trace amounts of the toxin on the lip of the bottle that could mix with the poured wine, tin and aluminum foils replaced lead wrappers by the 1990s.

CAVE

French for cellar. A cave is located at a wine producer where wines are stored to mature in barrels or in bottles. In Champagne, for example, the caves carved out of chalk are known as crayères, from the French word *cray* (chalk). These chalk caves maintain a constant temperature of about 43°F/6.5°C, which happens to be a perfect temperature for storing wine and champagne.

CHARACTER

The features of a wine that distinguish it from any other wine. Like people, a good wine should have character.

CHEWY

This wine term describes a red wine with a thickness and an abundance of tannins. A wine with this mouth feel will pour and taste viscous and thick and make the taster feel as though he or she could chew or mash the wine in his or her mouth.

COMPLEX

A wine with many facets. Having many different flavors and aromas. A fine wine is usually complex with many layers of flavors and aromas.

CO-OP

A farm, business, or other organization that is owned and run jointly by its members, who share the profits or benefits. In a winemaking co-op, the members are usually vineyard owners who deliver grapes to the co-op to be mixed with the grapes of other members and pressed to produce wines.

CORKED

Wine with the smell and taste of moldy straw or hay and sometimes damp mushrooms. It is caused by fungal infection of the cork.

CRÉMANT

Crémant is a sparkling wine processed using the traditional method. The grapes must be hand-picked and must be aged for a minimum of one year. There are seven Crémant appellations in France: d'Alsace, de Bordeaux, de Bourgogne, de Die, du Jura, de Limoux and de Loire.

CRISP

Usually associated with the slightly elevated acidity in wine and more often with white wine, denoting a fresh, firm, light character. Crisp white wines are usually unoaked; they are aged in steel or ceramic. Think green apple and light grapefruit but not lemon.

DECANT/DECANTING

Pouring wine from its original bottle into another container or receptacle (decanter), giving the wine a chance to mix with oxygen—to "breathe"—usually improving both its bouquet and taste. When you see the sediment is in the neck of the bottle, stop pouring. Once decanted, the wine is clearer and often smoother in taste.

DECANTER

A vessel whose function is most envied by the human stomach.
Ambrose Bierce

A special glass vessel used to separate the small amount of liquid containing sediment from the rest of the wine, usually reds. Use a clear decanter with no decoration to better see the level of sediment.

DELICATE

Light texture and subtle flavors. A delicate wine should not be paired with highly flavored foods. Refer to the chapter, "Food and Wine Pairing—It's All in the Sauce" on page 54.

DRY

Common wine term, a dry wine has little or no residual sugar left in it after fermentation. Dry wine has no perception of sweetness.

EARTHY

More often used to describe European wines, these have aromas and flavors resembling the earth, perhaps even soil or rock. Some Swiss white wines can be considered earthy.

ELEGANT

A stylish and refined quality found in a wine. An elegant wine is both complex and more often than not, expensive.

FAT/FLABBY

Fat or flabby refers to a wine with full body and light acid. The wine in this case tastes tired and flat.

FERMENTATION

The process of yeast acting upon the crushed grapes' sugar to produce alcohol and carbon dioxide. Without fermentation all wine would be sweet and alcohol-free.

FINISH

The final impression of the flavors a wine leaves in your mouth after you have swallowed or spat a mouthful of wine. See **long**.

FLORAL

Aromas found in wine suggesting flowers.

FORWARD

The dominant component in a wine that gives your mouth its first impression, for example, "fruit forward."

FRUIT/FRUITY

One of the wine descriptions used when a wine imparts prominent fruit flavors and aromas.

FULL-BODIED

A wine that fills the mouth with flavors and alcohol. A full-bodied wine is also considered "thick" or viscous, e.g., the reds from the northern Côtes du Rhône have a full body.

GLYCERIN

A complex alcohol that gives wine its thickness (chewy) or its viscosity.

HARSH

Too much acid or tannin describes these rough, biting wines. They generally lack fruit.

JAMMY

A wine rich in fruit but lacking in tannins.

KIMMERIDGIAN CLAY

A gray-colored, limestone-based soil originally identified in Kimmeridge, England. Kimmeridgian clay is calcareous clay made primarily of fossilized seashells. Mostly found in the Loire Valley, Champagne and Burgundy in France.

LEGS

These noticeable tears running down the inside of your wine glass after it's been tipped indicate the amounts of alcohol, glycerin and sugar. The longer the legs, the more alcohol, glycerin and sugar are present.

LONG

The quality of a wine after tasting or after being swallowed. The length of time a wine stays in the mouth after swallowing. See **finish**.

MAGNUM

A wine bottle holding twice the amount of wine (1,500 ml) of the average bottle (750 ml).

MELLOW

A way to describe smooth, soft wine with low acidity.

MERITAGE

A term used by California wine producers to describe their wines blended from Bordeaux varieties. It was at first designed to indicate a wine blend of higher quality than a common table wine. I love California Meritage and Bordeaux blends; they are true red nectars. Meritage is a Californian term and as such is *not* spelled Méritage with the French é.

MÉTHODE CHAMPENOISE

The traditional champagne method of making sparkling wine by allowing the second stage of fermentation to take place in the bottle.

MINERALLY

A term used when tasting wine, usually whites. It defines a sense or feeling of minerals in the wine, stemming from flavors of slate and schist. Examples of wines with a mineral note are Pouilly Fumé and Chablis.

MISTRAL

The Mistral is a strong, cold and dry regional wind in France, blowing in from the north or northwest. It passes through the valleys of the Rhône and the Durance Rivers to the coast of the Mediterranean, affecting the Languedoc and Provence regions.

MUST

The mix, prior to fermentation, of crushed grapes, skins, stems and seeds from which wine is produced, also known as pulp or pomace. These four components, along with the time they are in contact with the juice are critical to the final character of the wine. Must is not to be confused with the term musty.

MUSTY

Term usually associated with corked wine. The note is often described as a moldy cardboard or newspaper or a damp basement.

NOBLE ROT

A benign fungus that grows in warm, humid weather and concentrates the sugars of ripened white grapes. The must from these shriveled grapes becomes the finest sweet wine such as Sauternes from Bordeaux, Tokaji Aszú from Hungary and Spätlese level German Riesling. See **Botrytis cinerea**.

NOSE

A term very frequently used for the wine itself, the nose is simply the smell, aroma or bouquet of wine, as in having a "good nose".

NOTE

The word "note" can refer to the wine's aroma, flavor, or both, and is generally used to describe the more nuanced aspects of a wine's taste (floral, berries, vanilla, spice, etc.). Wine, like music, can contain more than one note, which together make up the wine's particular character.

NOUVEAU

A young wine meant to be consumed right away. It is French for "new", e.g., Beaujolais Nouveau.

OAK/OAKY

The smell, taste and character of a wine imparted by storage in oak wine barrels. Wines generally ferment in oak barrels or stainless steel. For inexpensive wines the wine maker may use wood chips or shavings, which are cheaper. Too much oak can impart unpleasant flavors.

OENOLOGY/OENOPHILE

The study of wine or one who studies and appreciates wine.

OXIDATION

The exposure of wine to oxygen or air. Some exposure is good and necessary, but too much will turn wine to vinegar.

PALATE

How an individual perceives the taste and flavor of wine in the mouth.

PÉTILLANT

The feeling of a slight prickle on the tongue due to the natural sparkle in the wine. Grüner Veltliner wines from Austria can show this character.

PHYLLOXERA VASTATRIX

The nasty little louse that destroyed European vineyards in the second half of the 19th century. It feeds on the roots and kills the vine.

PIPS/PITS

These grape seeds are a source of tannins in red wine. Pips can also impart a bitter taste, so the amount of contact they have with a juice must be monitored. Note that the twigs from the vines also contain some tannin. See **tannins**.

PLUMMY

Term used for big, round, red fruit reds.

POUILLY (FUISSÉ VS. FUMÉ)

Both are delicious but they are quite different. Try both. Pouilly-Fuissé is from Mâcon in Burgundy and is made from Chardonnay, while Pouilly-Fumé is from the Central Vineyards of the Loire Valley and is made with Sauvignon Blanc. There are also Pouilly-Vinzelles AC and Pouilly-Loché AC, both from Burgundy, which are very much worth a try.

PUNT

The indentation in the bottom of wine bottles. Some are clearly deeper than others, for example, Champagne bottles. Punts had the function of making the bottle more stable compared to a bottle designed with a flat bottom. A punt also increases the strength of the bottle, allowing it to hold the high  pressure of sparkling wine/champagne. One important point to note: that a larger punt indicates a finer wine is an old wives tale.

RESERVE, RESERVA, RISERVA

A term with no legal definition in the United States, it is implied that reserve wines are aged longer and are of higher quality than regularly bottled wines. The reserve wine may come from the best vineyards or the best barrels. In Spain and Portugal, *Reserva* is a regulated term for wines aged for at least three years in the cask and bottle, with a minimum of one year in cask. In Italy the wine must have aged between 27 and 60 months depending on the region. In Greece the wine must age three years. It should be noted that *Reserve* wines usually have a higher minimum level of alcohol.

ROBUST

Wines that are full-bodied, full-flavored and high in alcohol content.

SCHIST

A type of soil that crumbles easily and is found predominantly in vineyards in northern Rhône Valley and northern Alsace.

SEDIMENT

The non-liquid material at the bottom of a bottle of wine. Sediment is a combination of yeast, grape skins and other ingredients that can lead to an unpleasant taste. By removing the sediment, the taste of the wine is less bitter and the texture is smoother. See **decanter/decanting**.

SILKY

Having smooth texture and finish, silky wines lack tannins and have a fair amount of glycerin.

SMOOTH

A wine that feels good in the mouth, generally light in tannin and acid.

SOMMELIER

The wine specialist of a restaurant who has considerable wine knowledge and assists guests with their wine selection. A Sommelier usually works in high-end restaurants and helps you consult the wine list to best pair a wine to the meals you will be ordering.

SPICY

Having a nose and/or taste profile redolent of various spices, including clove, cinnamon, vanilla or pepper.

STALKY

An overly tannic wine. The name comes from the taste of the stalk or the stem of the grape, also stemy.

STEELY

The notes found in high quality Rieslings and some Chardonnays for their very dry flavor.

SULFITES

Sulfites are anti-oxidants and antiseptics and are absolutely necessary to protect wines, especially whites since they are usually in clear bottles. If you are asthmatic, please pay particular attention to sulfites in wine, as they can cause allergic reactions.

SWEET

Sweet is one of the wine definitions easily confused with fruity. Sweet indicates the presence of residual sugar, left over when the grape juice is converted to alcohol. Some dry wines have an aroma of sweetness that in reality comes from ripe fruit flavors.

TANNIN

An ingredient found naturally in the skins, seeds and stems of grapes. Tannins are usually found in red wines and give that dry, lip puckering sensation. Tannins are a very important component in red wine and soften with age.

TERROIR

The soil of the vineyard; the complete natural environment in which a particular wine is produced, including factors such as the soil, topography and climate affecting the final flavor of the wine. *Terroir* is perhaps most important in Burgundy, France. As noted by Andrew Jefford in his book *The New France*, "the aim of the *terroir* is to lend a sensual print to rock, stone, slope and sky." Henri Jayer, quoted in *Ode aux Grands Vins de Bourgogne*, J Rigaux (1997) shares that "The term terroir refers as much to climate as to the nature of soils and sub-soils. That's why we use the term '*climat*' in Burgundy..."

THIN

A wine with no depth. This type of wine is almost insipid with little character.

VARIETAL

Wine that is made from one dominant grape variety and whose label states so.

VELVETY

Another term for a smooth, silky wine with low acid, low tannin and substantial glycerin. See **balanced/elegant**.

VINICULTURE

The art of wine-making after the harvest.

VINTAGE

The year the wine is harvested and produced. A wine's vintage will be found on all wine labels. While an exceptional growing season can make for a great vintage, the perfect amount of sun and water, a well-timed harvest and quality ageing in oak, steel or ceramic also contribute to the overall taste of a specific vintage. Wine collectors pay special attention to the vintage, as value is based on the wine's ability to stand up to storage.

VINTNER

A winemaker. Louis Barruol from Château de Saint-Cosme says philosophically, "I don't like the word 'winemaker'. It doesn't mean anything to me. You make shoes; you don't make wine. I prefer to call myself a 'wine helper'. You help wine to make itself. That's how I consider my job…"

VITICULTURE

The art of growing grapes.

WINE PRESS

An ancient piece of equipment used for the pressing operation of separating grape juice or wine (must) from solids which may include seeds, skins and stems.

YEAST (BLOOM)

The organism that facilitates the process of fermentation and turns grape juice into alcohol. Yeast naturally grows on grapes and is known as bloom.

ZESTY

A wine with noticeable acidity and usually lemony, limey and grapefruit notes. An example of a zesty wine would be Sauvignon Blanc.

CONCLUSION

Ah! bouteille, ma vie, pourquoi vous videz-vous?
Molière

Molière's words, in English, mean, "Ah! bottle, my friend, why do you empty yourself?" Thank you for reading *My Wine Guide (made simple)*. I sincerely hope you enjoyed it and that your travels throughout the book gave you a sense of the multitude of climates, soils and grapes that are as close to you as your next glass of wine. I also hope that the next time you are browsing in a wine store, or reading a wine menu, that you will feel a greater sense of familiarity with what is before you and will be inspired to try something new. Should you have any questions or comments please contact me at mywineguidemadesimple.com.

Cheers,

Gérard Saint-Cyr

ACKNOWLEDGEMENTS

Men are like wine—some turn to vinegar, but the best improve with age.
Pope John XXIII

I wish to thank my parents for having been so demanding of me during my academic years regarding the art of communication. I hope, in your eyes, I met a fraction of your expectations. My boys for their quiet belief in me. Christine for her constructive suggestions. Günter, your help with regards to the German section is most appreciated. Catherine for showing me what it is to fight to the very end. Thank you to my father Gilles and to my friend Scot for allowing me to use their personal photos. I am grateful for the help of my dear friends Brad, Karl and Jerome for their unwavering support. My wordsmith Tamara Scott for your umpteen comments, questions and suggestions. To my editor, Shannon Saia, thank you for your solid organizational skills, editing and overall insight. Andriy, this would have been just another wine book without your tireless help and patience in creating the maps, labels and other images with me.

I wish to also convey my deep appreciation to the following wine professionals for their invaluable input regarding wine regions in the United States and Canada: Charles-Henri, Louise, Stephan, Tracy, Traci, Michaela, Mary Jane, Gillian, Michelle, Ron, Renaud, Christine, Marc, Jonathan, Jean-Marc, Ron, Nancy, Gladys, Stuart, Jenny, Tami, Megan, Taylor, Christopher, Peter, Heather, Andriana, Kate, Kim, Aubrey, Shannon, Judy, Charmaine, Jordan, Cori, Bob and Jane. Thank you *et merci!*

A heartfelt thank you to the Christian missionaries, French Huguenots and Catholic brothers for bringing grape vines into the United States, Canada and other countries around the world. Cheers to you all!

Last but not least, God for all of his strength.

SOURCES

In preparing this book, I spoke to a number of wine professionals at the following organizations.

United States

California Department of Food and Agriculture
California Grape Acreage Report of 2013
El Dorado Winery Association
Lake County Winegrape Growers
Livermore Valley Winegrowers Association
Lodi Wine Grape Commission
Mendocino Winegrowers
Monterey County Vintners and Growers Association
Napa Valley Grape Growers
Napa Valley Vintners
Oregon Wine Board
Paso Robles Wine Country Alliance
Russian River Valley Winegrowers
San Joaquin Valley Winegrowers Association
San Luis Obispo Wine Country Association
Santa Barbara County Vintners Association
Santa Cruz Mountains Winegrowers Association
Sonoma County Vintners
Sonoma County Wine Growers Association
Southern Oregon University

Temecula Valley Winegrowers Association
The Wine Institute of California
Washington State Wine Commission

Canada

Atlantic Wine Institute, Nova Scotia
British Columbia Wine Authority
British Columbia Wine Grape Council
British Columbia Wine Institute
Denmarc Vineyard, British Columbia
Grape Growers of Ontario
Jost Vineyards, Nova Scotia
L'Association des Vignerons du Québec (AVQ)
Vignoble de l'Orpailleur, Québec

ABOUT THE AUTHOR

Who does not love wine, women and song remains a fool his whole life long.
Johann Heinrich Voss

Gérard Saint-Cyr was born in Québec City and began his career in flavors and fragrances in Montreal and Toronto. Since his late teens, he has been intrigued with wine. He harvested grapes in Switzerland, visited vineyards, and attended wine tastings in numerous other European countries, Asia, Canada, Australia and the United States. After several years abroad he moved to the United States where he studied and taught wine theory and worked for a time as an independent wine broker. He holds four wine certificates from the United States and Switzerland. He continues to attend wine tastings and constantly reads about God's Nectar. He lives in New Jersey and occasionally sips a glass or two of fine wine while enjoying a glorious beach sunset.

BIBLIOGRAPHY

A glass of fine wine
An engaging book
A roaring fire
What more?
Gérard Saint-Cyr

"2012 Oregon Vineyard & Winery Census Report". Southern Oregon University Research Center, November 2013

"2013 California Grape Acreage Report". California Department of Food and Agriculture, 2014

"2013 New Zealand Winegrowers Labelling Guide". 22nd Edition, August 2013

"2014 Wine Statistical Information". ttb.gov, November 6, 2014.

"A Brief History of Wine". TheNewYorkTimes.com. November 5th, 2007

Ancient Peoples. "Roman Wine-making and its Uses". AncientPeoples.Tumblr.com September 28th, 2012

Anderson, Burton. *The Wines of Italy, An Endless Adventure in Taste.* Italian Trade Commission, 2006,

Baldy, Marian W., PhD. *The University Wine Course, A Wine Appreciation Text and Self Tutorial.* San Francisco: The Wine Appreciation Guild, 1997

Bastinaich, Joseph and Lynch, David. *Vino Italiano, The Regional Wines of Italy.* New York: Clarkson Potter, 2002

Beckett, Fiona. *How to Match Food and Wine.* London: Octopus Publishing Group Ltd, 2002

Broadbent, Michael and Duijker, Hubert. *The Bordeaux Atlas and Encyclopdia of Chateaux*. London: Segrave Foulkes Publishers, 1997

Camarra, Caroline and Paireault, Jean-Paul. *Wines of the World*. Goldalming, Surrey, U.K.: Colour Library Books, 1991

Casamayor, Pierre. *How to Taste Wine*. London: Hachette Livre, Octopus Publishing Group, 2001

Clark, Oz. *The Essential Wine Book, An Indispensable Guide to the Wines of the World*. New York: Simon & Schuster, 2001

Clark, Oz. *Wine Atlas, Wines & Wine Regions of the World*. London: Webster's International Publishing, 1995

Dickson, Paul. *Toasts, Over 1,500 of the Best Toasts, Sentiments, Blessings and Graces*. New York: Random House, 1991

Fielden, Christopher. *Exploring the World of Wines and Spirits*. London: Wine & Spirit Education Trust, 2004

OIV Statistical Report on World Vitiviniculture 2014

Gregt. "A Brief History of Wine Part III - Wine Storage - Barrels". Snooth.com November 9th, 2009

Guy, Patricia. "A Synopsis of Italian Viticultural History". PatriciaGuy.com 2010

Haapala, Kenneth A. "Wine 202: Adding a Bit of Scientific Rigor to the Art of Understanding and Appreciating Fine Wines." Journal Article from Washington Academy of Sciences.org

Jefford, Andrew. *The New France, A Complete Guide to Contemporary French Wine*. London: Mitchell Beazley, 2002

Johnson, Hugh and Robinson, Jancis. *The World Atlas of Wine*. London: Mitchell Beazly, Octopus Publishing Group, 2005

Kladstrup, Don & Petie. *Champagne, How the World's Most Glamorous Wine Triumphed over War and Hard Times*. New York: HarperCollins Publishers, 2005

LaMarca, George A. *Wine Wisdom, A Collection of Quotes, Toasts, Mirth and Merriment*. New York: Vantage Press, 2004

Matthews, Thomas. "The 1855 Bordeaux Classification". TheWineSpectator.com. March 29, 2007

McCoy, Elin. *The Emperor of Wine, The Rise of Robert M. Parker, Jr. and the Reign of the American Taste*. New York: HarperCollins Publishers, 2005

New York Wine and Grape Foundation. *The New York Wine Course and Reference*. New York: New York Wine & Grape Foundation, 2003.

Parker, Robert M. *The World's Greatest Wine Estates, A Modern Perspective*. New York: Simon & Schuster, 2005

Pellechia, Thomas. *Wine, The 8,000-Year-Old Story of the Wine Trade*. New York: Thunder's Mouth Press, 2006

Pellechia, Thomas. *Garlic, Wine and Olive Oil*. New York: Thunder's Mouth Press, 2006

Rainbird, George. *An Illustrated Guide to Wine*. New York: Harmony Books, Octopus Books Limited, 1983

Robinson, Jancis. *Vines, Grapes & Wines, The Wine Drinker's Guide to Grape Varieties*. London: Mitchell Beazly, Octopus Publishing Group, 2005

Robinson, Jancis. *The Oxford Companion to Wine*. City: Oxford University Press, 1999

Robyn. "A History of the Glass Wine Bottle". Wallafaces.com September 26, 2013

Simms, Cliff. "A Brief History of Roman Wine". TheExaminer.com January 5th, 2010

Steiman, Harvey. *Wine Spectator's Essentials of Wine, A Guide to the Basics*, New York: M. Shanken Communications, 2000

Taber, George M. *Judgment of Paris, California Vs. France and the Historic 1976 Paris Tasting that Revolutionized Wine.* New York: Scribner, Distributed by Simon and Schuster, 2005

Waugh, Alec. *Wines and Spirits*. New York: Time Life Books, 1968

Williams, Roger M. "Reims' Champagne Caves Chilled". TheWashingtonPost.com. November 19, 2006

"Wine-US Appellations of Origin". ttb.gov, October 14, 2014

Wines and Spirits, Looking Behind the Label. Wine & Spirit Education Trust, 2005

Made in the USA
San Bernardino, CA
20 February 2016